Here's what people are saying about
You Can Teach Someone to Read...

That Lorraine Peoples deeply believes that anyone can learn to read is evident not only in the broad scope of the material but also in the depth. Reading is essential in all walks of life and that it can be accomplished at any age is a strong message... This book is a valuable tool in helping those who have not yet adequately mastered reading skills.

> — Jeannine Stolaas, former junior high school educator,
> Sioux Falls, South Dakota

This is a must have book for anyone motivated to teach another to read. I honestly don't believe my children would be at their current levels of reading/comprehension without following this book. It has been a tremendous help and a definite 'on the first shelf' resource reference in our home. I've reviewed other reading selections, ...and by far I haven't yet seen anything that so simply and eloquently, with fewer words, helps a child get to where they need to be in reading and comprehension. Granted, people have used other methods and achieved just what I have, but I think this is an easier way to achieve it.

> — Amazon review by Angie, Homeschool Mom of 3, Hoover, AL

Peoples, who has devoted 33 years to teaching literacy, presents step-by-step procedures to give any adult the ability to teach someone to read. Of foremost importance, Peoples begins by encouraging readers to get to know their students. By providing the tools to identify a student's learning style, finding any physical learning blocks and encouraging family members to be involved in the reading process, instructors can encourage the student to continue learning. The remainder of the book has Peoples breaking down the mechanics of learning to read and gives very specific examples on how one could teach each of these concepts. Impressively, a person does not have to have a teaching background in order to execute what is being taught, making it a wonderful resource for anyone with the motivation to teach someone to read.

> — *Today's Librarian*, December 2000

**Today's Librarian, awarded *You Can Teach Someone to Read*
the best how-to book reviewed in 2000.**

I had the privilege of having Lorraine Peoples instruct struggling readers in my third grade English Language Development classroom, using her program from *You Can Teach Someone to Read*. The students were immediately drawn to the lessons because they were instructed at their level and moved at their pace.

A strength of this program is that after the initial assessment the instructor can address the learner's specific needs with the appropriate sections from the book. I found this program to be very effective with Hispanic ELL (English Language Learners) students.

Two valuable components of this program are the silly stories and the follow up activities. The silly stories provide a memory tool for the learners when they hit a stumbling block. I frequently overheard my students reciting the rules from stories when running into a word that they needed to decode.

The silly stories combined with the games engage even the most reluctant learners. The follow up activities reinforce the concepts and provide helpful visuals which the students can recreate to organize words into the various sounds made by the letters/letter combinations. After beginning instruction with Lorraine Peoples, students who at one time had avoided reading with the class became enthusiastic participants. I would recommend this book to anyone who is helping a struggling reader, or who is teaching a student with whom English is not his first language, or who is teaching beginning readers and feels that their current program is not meeting their students' needs.

— Andrea Dunne, 3rd grade ELL teacher,
Holmes Elementary School, Mesa, AZ

This book is an excellent supplement to our volunteer literacy program. The lessons, which feature approaches in whole language and phonetics, enable the tutor to draw upon quick strategies to bridge learning gaps in a variety of learning styles. The assessment areas are solid and provide for tutors to adjust lessons according to the pace of the learner.

— Coordinator of Volunteer Literacy Tutoring,
Clackamas Community College, OR

Even an adult can learn to read! *You Can Teach Someone to Read* has been instrumental in assisting me to teach a 42 year-old to read. The guidelines are concise and allow me flexibility in the design of my reading program.

— WYB, Amazon reviewer, Sept 2008

I am currently teaching an adult how to read. This book breaks down the rules of English for me. Once the adult grasps the rudiments of each letter and sounds it then opens a different world to the individual. This book frames each fundamental area that, as a teacher, you can quickly assess where the problem area is for the individual and teach someone to read.

— Maureen, an Amazon reviewer

This is the clearest and most comprehensive book on teaching reading I have read. It is very accessible and useful to both the teacher and the lay reader.

I just wanted to tell you that I love your book. As a former high school English teacher who now stays home with her three children, I found it interesting and enlightening. It really helped me to understand how someone learns to read, and I am looking forward to using your methods with my three and five year olds. I have been doing a lot of research on how children learn to read, and I found your book to be the most beneficial and informative book that I have read. Thank you for sharing your knowledge and expertise with others in the wonderful, easy to understand book.

— Cara Johnson, Sammamish, WA

I'm using *You Can Teach Someone to Read* with fourth through sixth grade at risk students. I want you to know they are learning to read. It works, and they like it.

— Reading specialist, El Paso, TX

You Can Teach Someone to Read provides a fun teaching method for phonics. I actually ordered another (more expensive) phonics program to evaluate alongside this one and ended up returning the other because it was difficult to follow. This book is easy to understand and the story method of presenting phonics rules is fun for the teacher and the student.

— An Amazon.com reviewer, 2009

I bought *You Can Teach Someone to Read* to teach an adult friend from another country. After a year, my friend is reading well. I'm not even a teacher, but I taught her to read with your book. It's wonderful. Thank you.

— Sandy, Phoenix

...I found much of the book to be useful and interesting. The "Silly Stories" were great and I think the children will enjoy them, as well as learn the rules being captured by them. I also liked the pictures, charts and tables scattered throughout the book as well as the materials included in the appendix.

I was worried about the emphasis on sight words, due to my bias against the "look-say" whole-word memorization-type reading programs. However, after studying Lorraine's list of words, I felt better about her rationale for their inclusion. Many of the words were ones I had recently told my own children that, "I can't explain why the word is pronounced like that since it violates everything we've learned, but please just memorize it and let's move on."

I would recommend, *You Can Teach Someone to Read* by Lorraine Peoples. I don't think you'll be disappointed. Also, if you just need a good reference book on phonics rules, this would b a good addition to your home library.

— Heather W. Allen, TOS Senior Analyst,
The Old Schoolhouse Magazine

It is so important to be sure early readers get the basic skills. Not only do we need to focus our attention on early readers but we must also help to raise the reading levels of the older child. Lay people, parents, friends, and teachers can all help achieve this goal using *You Can Teach Someone to Read*.
— *Arizona's Child*, May/June, 2000

This is a very good book which can help anyone learn to read. It provides very good guidance for someone who has not tutored reading before.
— R. Charles, Amazon.com reviewer, 2009

...presents a method for teaching reading, combining elements of memorization, phonics and whole language, which can be used to teach children and adults. Emphasis is on the basics of memorizing a sight vocabulary, phonics rules and comprehension skills. Silly Stories illustrate phonics rules. Includes step-by-step directions for facilitating teaching individuals or groups. The author has taught workshops for educators.
— Book News, Inc., Portland, OR

I am thrilled with this book's approach for teaching adults learn to read or to read better. I recommend it highly to anyone who has an opportunity to do this.
— Carol O. Allen, NC, an Amazon reviewer

You Can Teach Someone to Read by Lorraine Peoples may be the simplest and least expensive way to teach a child to read. Peoples, a longtime reading teacher, has put together a phonics-based tutoring plan to be used at home or in literacy programs. The daily lesson plans are detailed and very easy to follow. More than fifty phonics rules are presented as a silly story with word lists to practice for each. This book also concludes with reading comprehension skills, including understanding punctuation and contextual clues. Had this book been available when I was teaching my four to read, I would have tried this plan first.
— Debra Bell, author of *The Ultimate Guide to Homeschooling* page 121

You Can Teach Someone to Read has been a great resource for me as a first year kindergarten teacher. I needed some place to start. This book has been my teaching bible. Mrs. Peoples takes you right from the beginning of reading on through the scope to becoming a proficient reader. I have used her techniques for teaching sight words and phonics instructions. The Silly Stories are a great way to help children remember the rules. I shared this book with other teachers in my school. They now have copies of their own and are using them as much as I am.
— Penny Merchant, Bayfield, CO

A well-organized and presented 'basics' reinforcer.

— Eugene Schwartz, Editor at Large, *ForeWord Magazine*

...this book was written to equip any reader for the purpose of teaching someone else to read. ....this clearly-written, user-friendly guidebook provides any reader with a day-by day plan to teach phonics and reading comprehension to any student. Each lesson states at the beginning how long the author expects the lesson to last, then proceeds to give detailed procedures for each day. Of course each user can go at his own pace, but the sequential presentation of the lessons assure that the user will always know ....The author explains the importance of evaluating your student's progress as the lessons are mastered, and the evaluations are inserted where needed as the final step of the lessons....emphasis is on decoding, which gives the student the tools he needs to read most words in our language. Teaching the students to understand what they read is the goal of this book, and it reaches this goal in amazingly simple, yet thorough lessons that can be taught by anyone who can themselves read. A great deal is discussed in homeschooling circles about which phonics program to use, which songs and games work best, and which readers are most appropriate. This book cuts through all those accessories and provides a systematic blueprint that can be expanded on for all students, using all learning styles. With this book, you can teach your child, or any student, to read independently and confidently.

— Education Clearinghouse.org

I am tutoring an adult friend who is striving to learn English well enough to study for the U.S. citizenship exam. The lists of sight and phonetic words in the appendices are especially helpful.

— Ellie Maas, Chandler, AZ

I came upon a very interesting book, *You Can Teach Someone to Read* by Lorraine Peoples. It's a how-to book that anyone can use. Adult illiteracy is a big problem in this nation... She (Peoples) knows that everything that provides a decent life in this nation depends on the ability to read. So let's say you have a youngster who is having trouble in school. Now you can teach him or her yourself. Maybe there are adults in your family or just friends that need help? You can teach them, too. This truly is a gift that keeps on giving.

— Alan Caruba, Bookviews.com

Most of my teen age pupils have gaps in their reading and phonics skills, which have made their educational progress very difficult. This book has helped me target the areas where extra work is needed as well as giving me a good basic set of phonics rules to use in reviewing.

— Shelly Fletcher, reading tutor for teenagers, Laveen, AZ

...a must for anyone who would like to teach adults or children how to read or to improve rusty skills. It should be a must for classroom instructors, literacy programs and for parents to use at home to guarantee their children are not missing out. It is also ideal for friends who can use it to help someone who doesn't want others to know they cannot read. The author makes it fun to learn how to read.

— Sid Ascher, Syndicated Columnist for the
Current Newspapers, NJ

This gem of a book is a must for anyone who is trying to help someone else with their ability to read. It is packed with useful lists, clear diagrams, silly stories and funny cartoons. In a time of declining reading scores, this work fills a deep need in an entertaining way.

— Steve Nakamoto, author of *Men Are Like Fish*

YOU
Can Teach
Someone To Read

2nd EDITION

A How-to Book for Friends, Parents, and Teachers

Step-by-Step Detailed Directions to Provide

Any Reader the Necessary Tools to Easily Teach Someone to Read

LORRAINE PEOPLES

GLoBooks Publishing LLC
GILBERT, ARIZONA

Acknowledgments

Thanks to the many friends and family members who helped with the development and publishing of the revised version of *You Can Teach Someone to Read.* Special thanks to my husband, Graydon Peoples, who listened to me talk through every phase of the book, editing, researching, giving encouragement and advice; Sara Jackman whose financial help and faith in my mission made this project possible; my friends, Rusty Booth and Ellie Maas who edited for me and offered suggestions; and my brother, Richard F. Gulliver, who created the cartoons.

Thanks also to the knowledgeable, efficient team at About Books, Inc., who worked on the book's production, especially Cathy Bowman, Debi Flora, and Allan Burns.

Dedicated
to the students to whom I taught reading at
Grant Elementary in Des Moines, Iowa,
Glick and Fisher Elementary in Marshalltown, Iowa,
Phoenix Country Day School in Phoenix, Arizona, and
Tesseract School in Paradise Valley, Arizona.

to the individuals I have tutored,
including some enthusiastic third grade
ELL (English Language Learner) students
at Holmes Elementary in Mesa, Arizona.

and

to all those who will learn to read because
someone cared enough to teach them using
You Can Teach Someone To Read.

Contents

UNIT I: GETTING STARTED

UNIT II: BASIC PHONICS AND
THE MOST USED SIGHT WORDS

UNIT III: USING THE CONSONANTS AND VOWELS TO DECODE WORDS AND THE NEXT MOST USED SIGHT WORDS

Contents

UNIT IV: MORE OF THE MOST USED PHONICS RULES AND THE NEXT MOST USED SIGHT WORDS

UNIT V: DECODING LONGER WORDS USING SYLLABLE RULES, MORE SUFFIXES, COMPOUND WORDS, AND CONTRACTIONS

Birth of This Book

Readers have asked me, "Can you tell us the story about how and why you wrote *You Can Teach Someone to Read*? How did you get started, and how did you know what to put in it?" And so I will.

It took me thirty-three years to gain the knowledge I needed, and then several more years to put it on paper in a form usable for others. After the first edition was printed, I gave seminars, tutored those for whom English was a second language, instructed youth and adults how to teach reading, helped develop a reading program for the homeless, and answered questions asked through my website, www.youcanteachsomeonetoread.com. Then came a second printing. When it was time for the third printing, I realized there was still more information to be included in *You Can Teach Someone to Read*, and so the second edition came to be.

In the Beginning

Parents of my classroom students began to ask what they could do to help their children with reading other than read to them or listen to them read—especially something to help them recall the phonics rules. Consequently, I prepared a handout for them consisting of several pages. (Note: Most adults integrate the phonics rules as they use them and don't specifically remember them. Furthermore, many of these parents grew up when "whole language reading" was being utilized and probably weren't taught phonics when they were learning to read.) This handout was used for years by appreciative parents.

Strong Motivation

When I was considering early retirement to travel with my husband, the younger teachers let me know I couldn't leave unless I left them some rules about reading to guide them. I knew they came to me often, seeking knowledge about the phonics rules and the sequence for teaching them, but I didn't realize how much they depended on me. I told them I would develop a rules pamphlet for them, which would also include my "Silly Stories." (I always had fun with my students while teaching reading.) By this time, statistical research reported that many of our U.S. children were dropping out of school, and 43–46 percent of our fourth graders were ineffective readers. I believed I could and should help change this statistic. (Sadly, this statistic has not changed much over the decade.)

Traveling, Camping, and Writing

While traveling with our RV and boat, we met other travelers. When they discovered I was writing this book "on the road," they made their requests based on their experiences. First, it was non-reading adults—"Can they really learn to read, and how do I help them?" Next, it was, "I hope you're including how to work with kids before they get to school, so they'll have a good jump on learning how to read." After that, it was parents saying, "My child is in third grade and not reading well at all. I want to help, but I don't know how." And so it went. Each time, I answered, "Well, yes, that certainly could be in this book." The booklet I first set out to write became a full-fledged book, You Can Teach Someone to Read: A How to Book for Friends, Parents, and Teachers: Step by Step Detailed Directions to Provide Anyone the Necessary Tools to Easily Teach Someone to Read.

The Challenges

The first challenge was to include all the appropriate information to satisfy each group's needs. The truth is that basic reading skills are the same for all, regardless of age and regardless of who is doing the teaching. Thus, the book was organized to serve all age groups as well as individuals and groups. The next challenge was to remove the "educational lingo" and present the information in the clearest, simplest form possible.

Inspired by Teaching Experiences

I was assigned to teach grades in this order: second, sixth, third-fourth combination, fifth, second, first, first-second combination, second, first, and second again. (Nine of these years I also had administrative duties.) These assignments were in six different public schools and two private schools, all with varying economic environments. Over the course of my thirty-three years of teaching, the reading programs and techniques changed. All of this was an amazing and varied learning experience for me. At every grade and school there were readers of various abilities ranging from excellent readers to non-readers. From the beginning, I felt a mission to ensure that each student attained good reading skills, regardless of grade or environment. During that process, I learned how to determine learning styles, which of the phonics rules were true most of the time, and how to teach them so they would be remembered and utilized during reading. As I used this knowledge, it became obvious that students could get into reading more quickly. I realized that when a student accepts the fact that he needs help to read better and has the motivation to read, the process moves very quickly.

I remember one large, strong, well-liked fifth-grade boy who was the most graceful dancer I ever have seen but who could not read. We'll call him Chris. The class loved Chris, and after I read with the class the first time, I realized he couldn't read. After I had a personal conference with him, the class protectively informed me that he could not read. Teaching Chris became a class project. I told him I could teach him if he wanted to learn. Chris responded without hesitation that he wanted to learn to read. The class gasped. Since the class had initiated this task, I asked the students if they would be willing to help me teach him to read. They bargained. If he would teach them how to dance, they would help. He agreed immediately, but I didn't. It was my turn to bargain. "When he learns to read, we will have dance lessons every week for half an hour." After three months, he was reading third- and fourth-grade materials and often the geography book, which he loved. Dance lessons took place, but reading help never stopped. That experience was inspirational for me as well as motivational. I knew non-readers could learn to read.

Learning to Know the Student

Through many additional experiences, it was evident that a good reading teacher must observe students for physical and emotional problems that might affect their ability to read and then seek help for them if needed. I developed short mental checklists for myself to use for identifying physical and emotional problems.

Knowing how a student learns best was especially useful to me and appreciated by parents when I shared that knowledge with them. I felt that many of the students with learning problems were unable to learn in the particular manner in which they were being taught. For instance, teachers often have a visual learning style and so teach in a way that reaches students who learn best visually. If a student learns best by hearing or doing, he was often seen as a poor student. When teachers prepared techniques to reach visual, auditory, and kinesthetic learners, they became more effective teachers. I observed that many of the students learned better when we changed the teaching style for them. A tester of learning styles once told me I didn't need to have my students tested because I already had figured out their styles. My mental checklist was working well.

Therefore, the simple checklists I used to determine the physical and emotional problems of students and the ways to determine their learning styles are also included in the book.

How I Chose the Reading Skills to Be Included

Phonics and Sight Words

Extensive research indicates that phonics should be taught in a specific sequence, building on previous skills. I based the sequence in this book on that research. It also shows that phonics must be taught, along with sight words and other basic reading skills, in order for a successful reader to develop.

Knowing the alphabet letter names is a logical prerequisite to reading. Next, the sounds of the letters must be learned. Because many consonants have more than one sound, I first present the consonants that have only one sound and then the consonants that have more than one sound. I provide "Silly Stories," activities and games to make this learning more meaningful, fun, and lasting. One needs only to teach the letters and sounds students don't know. Interspersed with these lessons are other lessons for learning beginning sight words that need to be memorized. Learning the vowel sounds is vital to good decoding, so lessons about vowels are presented after the consonant sounds have been learned.

Edward Dolch and Edward Frye both researched and compiled a list of the sight words most often used. Frye determined that "over half of every newspaper article, every textbook, every children's story, and every novel is composed of the first 300 words on his list.

These 300 words make up 65% of all written material."

Most of the first three hundred words in the Dolch and Frye lists were the same, but there were some not common to both. I combined the first three hundred sight words on the two lists. Using this information, I analyzed those sight words with a vengeance.

What I Learned

1. Twenty-four percent of the words used most in writing were: "the," "and," "to," "is," "of," "a," "in," "that," "you," and "it." Although several of these words can be phonetically sounded out, I determined that because of their usage they should be treated as sight words (words that cannot be sounded out phonetically) and should also be the first sight words students memorize. A student should be able to name the written word within five seconds if he has learned them well.

2. When I further analyzed the sight words, I realized that many of them could be sounded out phonetically. I separated them from the list but kept them in order based on their usage.

3. Using the first one hundred words that could be sounded out phonetically, I figured out which phonetic rules were used in each word. I proceeded to do the same with the second and third lists of words.

4. Now I knew which phonetic rules were used most in the words used most often. This is the order they are now presented in You Can Teach Someone to Read. They are interspersed with the new sight words used most often.

5. I used this plan to teach school classes and individuals during tutoring. It was clear to me that students progressed very quickly when they were learning words they were seeing most often and applying the phonics rules, which, in turn, allowed them to decode new words. As they progressed, they read more difficult material easily. Their motivation was heightened because they were achieving their goal—reading.

Higher-Level Skills

After the phonics rules and sight words have been learned well, students begin a review session, which is built into the sequenced lessons, focusing on the vocabulary learned earlier. Continuing to build new skills by using a solid basic reading foundation is of utmost importance. Previously learned vocabulary is used while students also begin to decode longer words using consonant blends, suffixes, syllable rules, compound words, and contractions.

Strong emphasis is placed on making sense of the written word. The review includes higher-level skills, such as the use of punctuation, using context in reading, and learning comprehension skills. My favorite techniques are explained through actual exercises, with the expectation that the instructor will use the techniques over and over with the literature they select.

No literature selections are recommended in the book since I anticipate that instructors will know their student(s) well enough to select the appropriate reading materials.

My Joyful Confirmation

It is a joy for me to hear from folks from all over the world who are using *You Can Teach Someone to Read*. Comments have come from those teaching the young, rusty readers, teens, adults, and those for whom English is a second language. My final confirmation came when I learned that this program is being used overseas in educational institutions for instructing teachers how to teach reading.

Now that more than ten thousand first editions are being used, we have printed this second edition. Thanks to many of you, my personal mission of helping others teach someone else to read is on-going. Thanks also to those of you who are about to embark on the fun-filled, satisfying experience of teaching reading. I hope to hear from you, too.

—Lorraine Peoples

In a Capsule

This book was written because I strongly believe that:

- Any reader can help someone else learn to read.

- Teaching reading can be easy, fun, and satisfying for the student and the instructor.

- Reading with understanding is vital to a person's success; everything that provides quality living involves reading.

- The process and sequence for learning to read is the same for children, teens, and adults.

- Reading with understanding is not just memorizing, not just using phonics, and not just using whole language; it is rather a mix of the most important elements of all three.

- Most people who didn't learn to read well in the primary grades (for various reasons) want to be better readers but don't know how, so they have given up on becoming successful readers.

- There are teachers from several generations who didn't receive phonics instruction to prepare them for teaching reading and are now seeking that knowledge.

- A high percentage of adult readers don't remember the phonics rules because they have incorporated them into their reading. As a result, they feel inadequate to help or teach someone else to read.

This book is the result of:

- Analysis of reading based on research, experience, and knowledge gathered throughout thirty-three years of teaching reading to elementary children in public and private schools, training teachers, and tutoring individual children.

- Mentoring teachers.

- Helping the Phoenix, Arizona, Lodestar Resource Center for the homeless develop a successful, usable reading program for homeless adults.

- Training young people ages nine to eighteen to help another child to read better.

- Training adults to teach children and adults to read better.

- Volunteering as a reading tutor for students in a third-grade Hispanic ELL (English Language Learners).

- Providing international phone and email consultations concerning teaching strategies for individual and group reading concerns.

- Giving more than 150 seminars and book signings at bookstores, libraries, and events.

- Consulting with folks who are teaching reading and seek help with it.

This Book Is Based on Research

Research tells us the best ways to teach reading. Therefore, the material and lessons I've included are based on research. However, there is no discussion of reading theories or research included in this book.

- A 1993 Survey of Adult Literacy reported that in the United States ninety million (half of U.S. adults) are severely limited in their reading abilities.[1] Recent research indicates little change.

- Phonics is necessary for reading. "Beginning readers [should] be taught to sound out letters as the primary way to identify unfamiliar words," recommended a seventeen-member-panel of reading experts following a two-year study.[2] The Acting National Institute of Child Health and Human Development, after a thirty-year reading study, said, "There is no way to read if you are not very facile in the use of phonics."[3]

- A federally funded study at the University of Houston demonstrated that "intensive drills in phonics and the building blocks of words make young pupils into better readers."[4] "Reading gains for students taught the phonics way averaged twice those made by students using the whole language."[5]

- "For kids with reading difficulty, phonics—teaching children to read by having them associate letters with sounds—is an essential

---

[1] Palmaffy, Tyce. "See Dick Flunk." *Policy Review*, November/December 1997, Issue 86, p. 32.

[2] *New York Times*. "End 'reading wars' with hybrid teaching methods, report urges." *Minneapolis Star Tribune*, March 19, 1998, p. A15.

[3] Ibid.

[4] *Arizona Republic*. "Phonics drills best way to make kids better readers, study says." May 5, 1996, p. A26.

[5] Ibid.

component of reading instruction, since linking letters with sounds is one of their key weaknesses."[6]

This book's emphasis is on the important basic reading skills of:

- Memorizing a sight word vocabulary of words used most often, which can't be figured out by using the most commonly used phonics rules.

- Using the most common phonics rules to figure out words used most often, which don't need to be memorized, and obtaining a firm knowledge of how to apply those rules to unknown words.

- Developing basic comprehension skills to ensure that readers understand what the words are communicating.

—Lorraine Peoples

---

[6] Kiester, Edwin, Jr., and Sally Valente Kiester. "Does Your Child Have a Learning Disability?" *Reader's Digest*, August 1997, p.138.

UNIT I

GETTING STARTED

Motivation

You are reading this book because you want to teach someone to read—you are motivated. With this book, you will be a successful instructor.

To be a successful reader, the student must want to read. You may already have someone in mind, probably someone who is already motivated—who very much wants to know how to read.

Motivation is very important for *both* the person teaching and for the students who will learn to read. In this book you will learn new ways to teach and ways to help keep the student motivated. This book will give you what you need to teach someone to read.

As the instructor, you will help the students stay motivated to read when you follow the steps in this book. You will:

- Teach the student in the way he/she best learns.

- Involve the student, so he/she is helping himself/herself learn to read.

- Evaluate and teach the skills needed for reading.

- Provide experiences that show the importance of reading.

This book gives you some background information, ways to teach, and step-by-step directions using the most important aspects of reading. While teaching someone important to you how to read, you will have the satisfaction of watching that person develop reading skills and discover the joy of reading.

Find How the Student Learns Best

Each person learns best by seeing (visual), or by listening (auditory), or by doing (kinesthetic). These are called learning modalities or learning styles.

You, the instructor, need to know which way each student best learns. Observe each student carefully and fill out the following checklist. You may want someone else to observe as well.

Visual—By Seeing

The student:

____ Notices details such as jewelry or that a piece of furniture was moved.

____ Prefers to have pictures in books or magazines and looks at them carefully.

____ Watches and responds to facial expressions.

____ Becomes "glued" to the TV or game screen.

____ Makes an effort to see the person speaking.

____ Chooses to be in the front to watch a play, sports activity, or class.

____ Changes positions if the view is blocked.

____ Displays facial expressions that can be easily read.

____ Remembers after seeing information only once.

____ Writes a phone number or directions on paper rather than relying on memory.

___ Draws maps and diagrams to help remember.

___ Can picture things that were seen earlier.

___ *Total checks*

Auditory—By Hearing

The student:

___ Can listen to TV and concentrate on another activity at the same time.

___ Often remembers what was said the first time; doesn't need it repeated.

___ Often doesn't look at the person speaking.

___ Often hears a sound others didn't hear unless they made an effort.

___ Often has difficulty blocking out noise.

___ Is very sensitive to voice tones.

___ Is very sensitive to voice volume.

___ Enjoys talking.

___ Doesn't like to hear the same things repeated; may call it lecturing or nagging.

___ Repeats phone number or other information in order to remember.

___ Hums to self.

___ Can mentally rehear what was heard earlier.

___ *Total checks*

Kinesthetic—By Doing

The student:

___ Reaches out to touch objects, particularly in new situations.

___ Comments on how a specific texture feels.

___ Fidgets with whatever is close by when someone else is talking.

___ Can't listen for long times unless also doing something.

___ Changes positions, moves around more often than most.

___ Sits or stands close to others.

___ Touches, hugs, hits, snuggles, and pokes others more often than most.

____ Needs to be hugged, kissed, and snuggled.

____ Can recall how something was done by acting out those motions.

____ Will choose physical activity over watching TV or listening to a story.

____ Has a longer attention span when physically involved.

____ Wants to be shown how to do something rather than being told.

____ *Total checks*

Record the number of checks recorded in each of the following:

_____ Visual—Seeing

_____ Auditory—Hearing

_____ Kinesthetic—Doing

If one score has two or more checks than the other scores, that will be the student's learning style—the way the student best learns. If two scores are the same or only one check apart, the student best learns both ways. If three scores are the same or only one apart, the student best learns all three ways. Circle how your student best learns.

Most people have just one way they best learn, but some people have two equally strong ways. Even fewer people have three equally strong ways. How does your student best learn?

Now that you know how each student best learns, you will want to provide learning activities that use the way or ways the student best learns. Your student will still learn by the other ways but not as quickly or easily.

Have Someone Check Your Own Learning Modality

An instructor tends to teach the way he/she best learns. Therefore, you will need to have someone observe you so you will know how you best learn. If you learn best visually, and you are teaching someone who best learns kinesthetically, you will have to make more effort to teach kinesthetically.

When teaching a group of students, the instructor's lessons and activities must use all the modalities. Each student will then have the opportunity to learn through his/her learning style.

Find Possible Physical Problems That May Affect Reading

Observe students while teaching to determine if there is evidence of a physical problem that might cause reading difficulties. Record below each time one of the items in the list is observed.

While looking at written material the student:

____ Moves the *head* from left to right when following along on a page.

____ Tilts the head to one side or the other.

____ Squints the eyes.

____ Holds written material close to the eyes.

____ Covers one eye some or all the time.

____ Loses his/her place while following along.

____ Complains of tired eyes, itchy eyes, headaches, or a sick stomach.

If any of the above items are observed more than three times, it is possible a problem with eyesight may make reading difficult. Request the student be checked by an optometrist.

When speaking naturally the student:

____ Says letter sounds incorrectly.

____ Says words incorrectly.

____ Puts words in an unusual order in a sentence.

____ Confuses the short vowel sounds with each other.

If any of the above items are observed more than three times, it is possible a physical problem with speech will make reading difficult. Request the student be checked by a speech specialist.

When listening to someone speaking, the student:

____ Misunderstands what was said.

____ Asks to have it repeated.

____ Doesn't respond to the speaker unless looking at that person.

If any of the above items are observed more than three times, it is possible a physical problem with hearing will make reading difficult. Request the student be checked by a hearing specialist.

In normal situations the student is:

____ Withdrawn, doesn't want to participate in an activity.

____ Overly fidgety, active, and wiggly during lessons.

____ Nervous and tense.

____ Unprepared and does not finish assignments.

____ Forgetful of simple directions or information.

____ Confused when given more than one direction to follow.

If any of the above items are observed more than three times, it is possible an emotional or processing problem will make reading difficult. Request the student be checked by an educational psychologist.

Discuss the overall observations with adult students or with the parents of younger students. If necessary, request additional observation by an optometrist, speech therapist, hearing specialist, or educational psychologist. Often the local school or the state will provide these services.

Teaching and Relating to the Students' Learning Styles

Once a student's learning style is identified as Visual (seeing), Auditory (hearing), or Kinesthetic (doing), discuss the student's style with him. Below are some tips for using this knowledge.

If the student learns best by seeing (a visual learner), he will naturally observe every little facial expression the instructor makes to figure out how he is responding to him. This student will recognize smiling eyes or a smile as approval of what he's doing and will be encouraged to continue. If he sees a frown, however slight, the student will look away from the instructor, turn away, or otherwise distract himself. He may show discomfort or have a head-down pouty look. If that happens, the instructor should acknowledge the feelings and talk to the student.

When you instruct this student, use materials that provide a visual impact, such as objects and a variety of colors. Pictures, videos, TV, and observation activities are also effective tools for teaching him. During quiet study time an environment that provides a low visual impact is best. Images such as moving objects, moving people, vibrant colors, and busy bulletin boards can distract the student from concentrating.

If the instructor is a visual learner, as most people are, he must be very aware that he naturally sends facial and bodily messages, both positive and negative. He will easily be able to read the student's facial and bodily expressions to figure out how he is responding to the instruction. If the instructor a not a visual learner but his student is, the instructor will need to study the student's facial and bodily expressions to see how he's responding. Because the student needs visual clues from the instructor, he will also deliberately need to send visual messages through facial and bodily expressions.

If the student learns best by hearing (an auditory learner), he will be very sensitive to the instructor's voice tone and inflections. If the student hears a firm voice or a voice with a raised pitch and/or volume, he may sense or decide that the instructor is angry or frustrated with him. When he hears a voice expressing pleasure, he will be encouraged and feel the instructor is pleased with him. If the instructor repeatedly corrects or tells the student what to do, he may feel he is being nagged and "turn the sound off." Think of this student as having a tape recorder in his head. He will hear what has been said over and over, even after the lessons or comments are over. Even something the instructor might have thought he didn't understand will "replay" for him later, and he'll "get it." This student doesn't have to look at the person speaking to understand what he is saying. If he hears the instructor's voice tone criticizing another student, he can retreat emotionally. He often has the ability to hear someone mutter or speak in the adjoining room when others don't. He may hum or sing to himself, spell words to himself before writing them, or repeat what was previously taught when doing homework. These are coping skills for him but may be distractions for some others in the class. He can concentrate even when there is activity around him. However, he is highly distracted by the noises around him since he even hears background noises such as fan motors, a dog barking in the distance, or a clock ticking. A person who is not an auditory learner might not be aware of those noises. Effective instruction for the auditory learning student includes minimal verbal repetition, use of music or songs that teach, listening to books using earphones, and having a quiet work space.

If the instructor is a visual learner, it may bother him that the student doesn't always look at him when he is speaking. The instructor should explain to the student that he knows the student learns best by hearing. He should tell the student that many people, himself included, learn best by seeing and need to have others look at them when they are speaking or listening. Learning to look at people when they speak is a polite social skill. The student will need gentle assistance to develop this skill. If the instructor is an auditory learner, he has experienced many of the pains and frustrations that this student in a school setting has to cope with. He is a lucky student if his instructor is also an auditory learner—he will be understood.

If the student learns best by doing (a kinesthetic learner), he will seem to have some part of his body moving constantly. He'll be a wiggler, a toucher, and want to be close to another person whether that person wants it or not. He'll drum his fingers, rock, frequently switch positions in a chair, and often appear to be inattentive. He will become weary of being told to sit or stand still. He probably enjoys physical activities, such as sports, outdoor activities, dancing, crafts, and building.

The instructor should tell the student that because he learns best while being active that doing something active will help him understand his lessons—like writing, drawing, mapping, building, or acting. The instructor should also tell the student he'll try to teach him in the way he learns best sometimes but that the student will also have to practice listening without wiggling or touching someone else. The instructor may give him a motive such as, "Others will accept and like you better if you can sit still and listen—it's a good social skill to learn." Let him know that his wiggliness may prevent others as well as himself from learning well. The instructor should devise lessons that involve bodily activity, such as "I'll say a word; if you hear the short sound of 'i' in the word, stand up." Allow the student to take an active part in the lessons. If the instructor is giving a lesson on paper, give the student a pencil or crayon to use. If you are using a lesson printed on a transparency, give the student a temporary marker to use—that's usually a different tool for him and he feels very special. Give him specific directions, such as underlining vowels on a printed page as you say the words, or have him draw the whiskers on a picture of a cat. If wiggling is preventing his ability to listen, give him something to hold and feel while he listens, such as a roll of masking tape.

The Instructor's Magic Solution

For the Tutor—Because a tutor teaches individual students, he can and should present the lessons in the student's learning style or styles. Many tutors have multiple students, however. While the temptation is to use the same lesson again, the best tutor will redesign the lesson to fit each student's learning style.

For the Classroom Teacher—This instructor will prepare each lesson so it has elements in it for each of the learning styles. Research shows us that the best classroom teachers teach to all learning styles regularly by incorporating seeing, hearing, and doing. Individual students who require it can be provided with individual help tailored to their learning styles.

Get to Know Your Student's Interests

Get to know your students. Find out through casual conversation what interests each student. It's OK to share some of your interests also. Gather information about the following as early as possible:

- hobbies
- sports
- jobs
- places he/she likes to visit
- family
- music
- places he/she wants to go
- friends
- favorite foods
- pets and animals
- favorite TV shows
- favorite movie
- favorite thing to do when alone
- favorite thing to do with friends
- dreams for the future
- favorite table games
- what he/she wants to know more about
- what he/she wonders about
- other information

You can use the information you learned about your student to provide additional reading experiences, such as a trip to the library, making a reading game, reading a book together, looking up information, and so forth.

Get the Family Involved

The Younger Student

The younger student should be read to three or more times a week. It is important to read and sing nursery rhymes and books with rhyming words to preschool-age children. Help your preschool child discover letters and their sounds using objects, familiar signs, cereal boxes, and TV programs designed for younger children. As a child begins to read he/she will also want to take turns reading with an adult. This should be encouraged until the child reads fifteen to thirty minutes a day to someone outside of school or independently. Adults should continue to read to the young child even after the child is able to read. They still need to hear the written word read aloud. It helps build the speaking vocabulary and helps develop a love for books and reading.

Some of the activities listed below for the older student are also good for those younger.

The Older Student

Older students who have or haven't yet learned to read also need to be read to. Instructors must acquire written material that is of special interest to the student. Reading should be relevant to their everyday lives. For instance, if the student is interested in sports, use trading cards, newspaper sports pages, sports magazines and books. If the student is interested in foods, gather menus, recipes, and food containers.

There are several ways to read to and involve older students. Many of these also work with younger students.

1. The student may whisper or echo read along with you or a small group that is reading aloud. Brief discussions should occur fairly often to assure the reading is meaningful.

2. The student may follow the written words of a song that interests him/her while listening to the singing.

3. The student may follow the written word while listening to a book or article that has been tape recorded. The student may also read along with the tape.

4. The student may watch a video, TV show, or video with captions.

5. The student may follow the words as you read poetry by writers such as Shel Silverstein (available at public libraries). These poems are usually so well liked, they can be read over and over. Eventually, students will read the poem with some help and finally, on their own.

6. Instructor and student may tape record a child's book with lots of speaking parts. Give the tape and book to a child to enjoy. Enjoy reading along with the book as the child hears it the first time. Make this type of reading an ongoing project. This activity gives the student a feeling of pride and practice on basic sight words.

7. Make games based on the student's interest or based on favorite table games. Put the sight words or skills the student is working on into the games. For example:

   a. Working on sight words. Base the game on the rules of Old Maid. Use a set of baseball cards and make a set of question cards. On each card, write a question that uses sight words the student is working on. The question's answer can be found on one of the baseball cards. A set is made by matching the baseball card to the question. The question and answer must be read before the set counts.

   b. Working on contractions. Base the game on the rules of Memory. Choose twelve contractions to use for each game set. Make twenty-four cards for each game set. On twelve cards, write the first word of each contraction; on the remaining twelve cards, write the last part of the contraction (*would* and *n't*). Match two cards to make a set, say the contraction, and take another turn.

c. A construction worker needs to read job directions.

Make the Game. Have the student help make the game. Find a large picture or blueprint of a house and paste onto cardboard. Number twenty different areas on the house in the sequence the house would be built. Write two identical direction cards to go with each numbered area, for example, "nail 3/4-inch plywood onto floor joists."

Object of Game. The object to the game is to complete the house first.

Set up the Game. Shuffle the cards and deal five to each player. The remaining cards are placed in the center. There will also be a discard pile in the center, as well as one in front of each player. The player moves his/her marker in sequence from area one through area twenty, as he/she gets the correct direction card. The player must read the direction card before his/her marker can be placed. All cards discarded are "dead" and may not be picked up by either player.

Play the Game. If the first player has the direction card for area one on the center discard pile, he/she reads the card directions aloud and places his/her marker on area one. If the player also has the direction card for area two, he/she reads it aloud and places the marker on area two. The player will continue to put down in order and read as many direction cards as he/she can. If the player uses all five cards, he/she may draw five more and continue to play. When the player can't play, he/she chooses one card from his/her hand to place in a discard pile. After the player's turn, he/she draws to bring hand up to five cards. It is the second player's turn, who follows the same directions as above. When the cards in the center pile are gone, all cards in discard piles are shuffled and placed in the center pile. Play resumes.

8. Engage in activities that require everyday reading, such as menus, medicine directions, traffic signs, cleaning and garage supplies, recipes, food labels, poison warnings, and so forth.

9. List specific questions or subjects of interest to the student, then go to the library. Together use the card catalogue or computer to locate resource material, find the books, and check them out. Use them together to find answers. Teach that a table of contents

is usually in the front and tells what broad information is in the book and on which page it begins. Teach that an index is usually in the back of the book and tells what specific items are in the book and on which page to find it. Repeat this process often.

10. Read from computer programs that are of interest to the student.

11. Read comic books.

12. Read material relating to a job the student may have.

13. Read how-to-directions that relate to the student's interests, then together follow the directions.

Teaching Reading in English to Students Who Speak Another Language

Below are some basic considerations an instructor should be aware of when teaching reading in English to students who speak another language. A short discussion of what each consideration means to the reading instructor is in the box below each point.

1. The student will progress best if he already understands what is spoken to him in English and can speak in English at a beginning level or more.

Strive to create a warm, positive environment so the student will feel comfortable learning to read in English. As you move through the lessons in the order they are presented, you will find the student will not understand the meaning of every word. Before he will let you know he doesn't know what a word means, he needs to feel confident that you will accept his lack of knowledge and help him learn the meanings. He needs to know it's all right to ask what a word means. Take time to make sure he understands the word, hears it in a sentence, and can use it in a sentence. Make the word meanings and sentences relevant to your student's experiences. Introduce a dictionary when you feel he's ready. If he wants to use it, put it into your lesson plans sometimes.

2. How well the learner speaks and understands English will highly correlate with the speed with which he learns to read and comprehend well in English.

> The more a student understands the English language, the more quickly he will move through the lessons. The most commonly used phonics rules and sight words are placed in the lessons based on the order they're most often used in writing. These lessons build on each other so the student can read books of interest or material relevant to his daily life.

3. Research tells us that teaching only in English to a learner whose first language is not English will ensure faster learning.

> Do not allow any conversations in your student's first language any of the time when he is with you. Keep your student focused on English only. This sounds tough, but it will pay off. If it seems too difficult, practice short direction sentences using the sight words, such as "Please go get the book" or "Thank you for getting the book." Body language, such as gestures, pointing, and facial expressions are okay to use as cues.

4. The basic reading skills needed for successful reading in English are the same basic skills required whether or not the student's first language is English and regardless of his age.

> There will usually be some phonics rules and sight word vocabulary that the student always knows. There will also be new information to learn. Evaluation checks need to be constantly underway through observation or paper/pencil exercises to make sure the basic skills are well learned and as the lessons proceed. You Can Teach Someone to Read will be effective for teaching anyone to read, regardless of his age or language.

5. When a student is learning new reading skills in a language different than his first language, more repetition is normally required.

> Patience is the magic key word for the instructor. Learning a new skill of any kind requires at least five to ten repetitions and practice. For instance, your student may need time to think in his first language in order to recite a sentence using a specific sight word. Allow him the time to think. Observe and record the skills and sight words that are more difficult for him. Develop an activity that would allow him to have additional practice but in a different way.

6. Some languages use the same letters as English, but that is not always the case. It is important for the instructor to know that the student recognizes each letter, both upper case and lower case.

> Quick early evaluations are provided for the instructor in Unit II. Don't assume the student knows a skill. Evaluate it as instructed. If the evaluation shows he already knows a skill, the instructor can say something like, "You already know this. Good for you. I won't need to teach them to you. Let's find out what else you know and what I need to teach you." Usually, the student will react with a glow and a smile.

7. Consonant letters in some languages have only one sound. In the English language most consonant letters have only one sound—until they are combined with a second letter. Sometimes those combinations make a totally new sound.

> It may seem strange and difficult to learn, but it is important for your student to recognize it and to learn the rules. For instance, the letter "c" may make an "s" sound as in the word "cent," or it may make a "k" sound in "cane." An "s" combined with "h" will make a totally new sound as in "sh." For instance, one "Silly Story" helps the student learn the sound of "sh." All ages love these stories and use them as a memory crutch, as do younger students.

8. Vowel letters in some languages have only one sound. In the English language all vowels have more than one sound and have yet more when combined with certain other consonants or other vowels.

Knowing the different individual vowel sounds and the sounds of combinations of vowels is an extremely important skill for the student learning to read in English. This amazing skill gives him the ability to figure out unknown words easily.

9. Word meanings and the structure of phrases and sentences can often be quite different in English than in the learner's first language.

Patience and practice will be needed in order for the student to become accustomed to the structure of the English language before solid comprehension is achieved. Even though there is some help included in this program, much of this information will be learned through your communication with each other. Try speaking in sentences rather than in phrases.

General Procedures for Instructing Lessons in This Book

Repeat, Repeat, Repeat—
So the Student Will Remember

This book will have some repetition built into the lessons, but it is up to the instructor to be sure the material will be repeated at least five times in ways that will be interesting to students.

You should get the students to help develop games, activities, and find information that will give more practice. This will let them know they can help themselves to learn. Do this as soon as possible after you start the lessons.

Give the student homework that lets him/her repeat, such as:

1. Read to someone.

2. Listen to someone read.

3. Listen and read along with a tape, video, song, or computer program.

4. Tape a book along with another adult.

5. Find objects that begin with a certain sound.

6. Play a reading game (that you and the student have already played together) with someone else.

7. Hunt for street signs. Keep track of how many signs said stop. Think of other words that rhyme with "stop."

Think of other homework that is age-appropriate for the student, provides practice for what you have taught, and gives the student the needed reading repetition. This will become easier after you have worked with the student several weeks. You will know what activities he/she likes and needs and what his/her interests are.

Procedures for Instructing a Group

Instruct the whole class at the same time. Use an overhead projector for group reading instruction, which will allow you to face the students and interact with them. Everyone will be able to see well because the image on the screen is large. Everyone can see your facial expressions and the way you use your mouth as you teach phonics, making it easier for students to hear what you say. Observe students and determine if something needs to be reworded or retaught. Also evaluate each student.

Although some students learn faster than others, all will need to review. Those still learning will benefit from the students who are reviewing. Work additionally with a small group or with individuals to provide repetition for those who need it.

When preparing the lesson, write the word "lists" with permanent overhead markers. Use temporary overhead markers for marking while teaching. Wash the transparent sheet with cool water following the lesson. The lesson you wrote with permanent ink will stay and what was written with the temporary ink will disappear. Dry the transparency with a soft rag or paper towel. The transparent sheet should be filed for reuse another time.

Procedures for Instructing an Individual

Follow the instructions above. An overhead projector is not necessary. It is, however, worthwhile to use the transparent sheets placed over a white or light-colored piece of heavy paper. It's also good for the student to take a turn using the temporary pen on the transparency while learning the information.

Evaluating and Instructing Sight Words and Consonant and Vowel Sounds

Of the words most often used in written material, about eighteen out of one hundred are words that cannot be phonetically figured out. They are called sight words because they have to be learned by sight—memorized.

Of the words most often used in written material, about forty-seven out of one hundred are words that can be read by using basic phonic rules.

Of the words most often used in written material about thirty-five out of one hundred words are longer words or words not used as often. They can be learned by breaking the words into parts or by using context reading.

As you follow the lessons in this book, you will teach your students:

- The words that must be memorized, called sight words.
- To find phonetic patterns and determine the phonics rules.
- To use phonics rules to figure out short words.
- To figure out longer words using the phonic patterns and rules.
- To figure out an unknown word by using the words around it—context reading.

Evaluate Student Knowledge

The reading lessons in this book will ask you to evaluate what your students already know and don't know. Don't assume they know something. When a student is reading with difficulty, it is often because mastery of one or more of the beginning reading skills is missing. Follow each step in every lesson. When the book asks you to evaluate, do it. Again, *don't assume the student already knows it.*

Get a pencil and do the following activity.

1. Draw a picture of a ladder with ten rungs, resting against a tall house.
2. Draw the picture of a person with a book in the upstairs window.
3. Draw a person by the ladder.

Now think of the ladder as the way to climb to independent reading.

1. Label the rungs of the ladder "reading skills."
2. Label the person in the upstairs window "independent reader."
3. Label the person by the ladder "reading student."

The person in the window is where the person by the ladder wants to go.

1. Erase four of the rungs.
2. Label the missing rungs "missed school days."

Now study your picture. Can the reading student go up the reading skill rungs on the ladder to get to independent reading? Well, maybe, but certainly not easily or quickly. And if your picture showed missing rungs one after the other, it would be almost impossible to climb! The ladder would give the same trouble every time it was used.

The ladder with "missed school days" happens when a young student in first, second, or third grade has been absent due to an illness of a week or more. Often the reading skill that was taught during the young student's absence has not been learned very well or maybe not at all.

A vital part of your job as the reading instructor is to evaluate and find the "missing rungs" or reading skills not mastered. Once you know which reading skills were not learned, your job is to teach those skills again.

Now go back to your picture. Draw in the rungs that were missing. See how easy it is now for the reading student to climb the ladder?

The reading student already had some of the reading skills on the ladder; so when you filled in those missing skills, the progress to the top of the ladder, becoming an independent reader, will be rapid.

Your job is to evaluate carefully in order to find the missing reading skills and teach them as well as the new skills. When this book asks you to evaluate, do it. Your student's reading success may depend upon it.

UNIT II

BASIC PHONICS AND THE MOST USED SIGHT WORDS

Upper and Lower Case Alphabet Letters Recognition Evaluation

Evaluate the student's ability to name all the *upper and lower* case alphabet letters.

*A a, B b, C c, D d, E e, F f, G g, H h, I i, J j, K k, L l, M m,
N n, O o, P p, Q q, R r, S s, T t, U u, V v, W w, X x, Y y, Z z*

Procedures

1. Buy or make one set of upper and lower case alphabet letters such as those written on colorful cards or tiles without pictures or made of felt, wood, foam, rubber, baked dough, or magnets.

2. Spread the alphabet letters randomly on the table or floor.

3. Ask the student to pick up the letters one at a time and name the letter.

4. Put the letters named correctly in one pile.

5. Record the results, so you know which ones to teach.

Together, count how many letters the student already knows. Tell the student you will help him/her learn the others. Go to Section 2.

Phonics Evaluation: Consonants With Single Sounds

Evaluate the student's ability to say the following single consonant letter *sounds*:

Bb, Dd, Ff, Hh, Jj, Kk, Ll, Mm, Pp, Rr, Tt, Vv, Zz

Instructor Background

All the alphabet letters except the vowels *Aa, Ee, Ii, Oo,* and *Uu* are consonants. When the name of the consonant letter is said, some part of the mouth has to touch another part of the mouth for the letter to be a consonant. Of the twenty-one consonant letters, thirteen have single sounds. The other eight consonants have more than one sound. *Yy* and *Ww* are a consonant and vowel, but are a consonant most of the time. Knowing the sounds of the consonants helps the reader to figure out unknown words.

The *single consonant letter sounds* have the first sound heard in each of the words below:

Bb as in <u>b</u>oy	*Dd* as in <u>d</u>og	*Ff* as in <u>f</u>un
Hh as in <u>h</u>ello	*Jj* as in <u>j</u>ello	*Kk* as in <u>k</u>itten
Ll as in <u>l</u>ion	*Mm* as in <u>m</u>an	*Pp* as in <u>p</u>et
Rr as in <u>r</u>un	*Tt* as in <u>t</u>oy	*Vv* as in <u>v</u>iolet
Zz as in <u>z</u>oo		

Procedures

1. From an alphabet set, take the upper and lower case alphabet letters and spread them randomly on the table or floor:

    Bb, Dd, Ff, Hh, Jj, Kk, Ll, Mm, Pp, Rr, Tt, Vv, Z z

2. Ask the student to pick up a letter and say the sound it makes.

3. Put the letters for which the sound was said correctly in a pile.

4. Record the results so you know which ones to teach.

5. Together count how many the student already knows. Tell the student he/she knows quite a few and you will help him/her learn the others.

If the student didn't easily recognize all the upper (capital) and lower case (small) alphabet letters and/or couldn't give the letter phonetic sounds of the above letters, go on to teach Section 3 and also start Section 4.

If the student did easily recognize all the upper (capital) and lower case (small) alphabet letters and could give the letter phonetic sounds of the above letters, go directly to Section 4.

Phonics Instruction: Upper and Lower Case Alphabet Letters Evaluation and Consonants With Single Sounds

Help the students learn upper and lower case alphabet letters and the following single consonant sounds not previously known:

Bb, Dd, Ff, Hh, Jj, Kk, Ll, Mm, Pp, Rr, Tt, Vv, Z z

Procedures

Choose from the learning activities and lessons below to teach the consonant letters and sounds. Individuals who have not learned a lot of letters should receive additional individual instruction and game-type activities.

1. Have the students name words that are important to them. These might include family names, hobbies, sports, foods, and so forth. With a colored marker, write each word on a large file card. These cards will be useful for many learning activities. Students may choose to put a picture on each card, but it's not necessary. Using the letters each student needs to learn, have the student locate all of a specific letter (for instance, the *B, b*s) in the words, listening to the sound in the words as you and students say the word. Continue through all the letters the students should learn.

2. Make two cards of each unknown letter. Play the matching game Concentration or Memory using the cards. As a card is turned over, the player must name the letter and its sound before the second card may be turned over.

3. Make up a scavenger hunt based on the student's interest and letters that need learning. On a paper draw or paste a picture of something the student is interested in. Put the letters the student needs to learn on the picture. For instance, a train, with a letter on each car in the train. Provide a place and time limit for the student to locate real objects that have the letter sound in it. When all objects are located or the time is up, have the student name the object, the letter it represents, and the letter sound.

4. Make up other activities that involve being active, using objects and sound. Have fun with the students.

If an individual student continues to have difficulty learning many letter names and sounds, consult with the parents and work together to determine what the student's stumbling block might be and what other means might be taken to help the student, such as getting professional evaluators.

The problem could be the readiness level, hearing, eyesight, health, worry, a learning disability, or something more obscure. Sometimes a more thorough check by a learning specialist or a medical doctor is an important first step toward helping the student learn to read.

Sight Word Evaluation

Evaluate the beginning sight word knowledge with each student.

Instructor Background

Sight words are words that cannot be "sounded out" or "decoded" by using the most common phonic rules. Sight words must be installed in the memory bank for instant recall.

The ten sight words below make up about 24 percent of all written material. These ten words are best memorized, although a few of the words can be decoded by using the phonic rules. The student should have *instant* recall of each word.

Procedures

Write the following words on a list or on cards. Check each child individually. Allow the student five seconds to say each word. Record the responses for future use. With the student count how many words he/she already knows. Tell the student you will help him/her learn the words he/she didn't know.

the	and	to	is	of
a	in	that	you	it

If the student doesn't have instant recall (each word named within five seconds), read Section 5, General Procedures for Instructing Sight Words on pages 41 to 42 and then go on to SECTION 6, page 43.

If the student does have instant recall (each word named within five seconds), read Section 5, General Procedures for Instructing Sight Words on pages 41 to 42 and Section 7, General Instructions for Reviewing Sight Words on pages 45 to 46. Then go to Section 8, page 47.

General Procedures for Instructing Sight Words

Print the sight words on an overhead transparent sheet. Project onto a screen, using an overhead projector.

The lessons should move quickly to keep the student's attention. Always use a finger, pointer, or hand, sweeping from left to right under each word as the student says it. You say a word, the student repeats, you say the next word, the student repeats, and continue through all the words on the list. If you hear a word misspoken, simply repeat the word, then have the student repeat it.

Repeat each word a minimum of five times during each initial lesson in order to give the student a chance to memorize. Before information is *well* learned, it must be repeated at least five times within a relatively short time. Information will be remembered even better if it is repeated using the way the student learns best.

Below are some suggestions for providing additional repetition using the overhead transparency.

If instructing a group:

1. Quickly say the word, then have the students repeat.
2. Do the same thing but more quickly.
3. Point randomly to the words and ask those wearing red (or any classification) to say the words.
4. Have brown-eyed students say the word with you; blue- and green-eyed students repeat.
5. Point to the words randomly; you and students say the word.

If instructing an individual:

1. Say the word quickly, student repeats.
2. Do the same thing but more quickly.
3. Have student point to words he/she can say and say them. You repeat.
4. Point to the words the student omitted and say them. Student repeats.
5. Point to the words randomly, you and student say the word.

Sight Word Instruction

Procedures

Follow Section 5, General Procedures for Instructing Sight Words on pages 41 to 42.

Sight Words to Memorize

the	and	to	is	of
a	in	that	you	it

Additional Activities

These will help students learn these words and also review the more difficult letter sounds that were previously taught.

1. Make a game of Concentration.

2. Make a game based on other favorite card games such as Fish, Old Maid, Spoon, or Hearts. If possible, incorporate a subject matter the student likes or that is currently being studied.

3. Read something of high interest to the student while using the hand to sweep under each line. The student listens and watches for only one of the sight words, such as "the." Using a highlighter pen, the student or teacher marks the word. Reread the story and tape record it. Use your hand to sweep under each line. When the word "the" is in the story only the students say "the." Play the story back and have the students follow along using the book.

4. Repeat the third activity above, but use another sight word and a different color for highlighting. Reread and record with the student

saying *both* sight words. Repeat the process each day with new words.

5. Create your own activities.

When the student has instant recall of the sight words in this section, read Section 7, General Procedures for Reviewing Sight Words, below, and then go to Section 8, page 47.

General Procedures for Reviewing Sight Words

For each set of ten words, there will be at least two review lessons during the week. Below are some suggestions for providing additional repetition. Use one to three activities each day, depending upon your student's needs. Continue to use the same overhead transparency used for the first lesson, cleaned if necessary. Remember to keep the lessons short and moving quickly.

If instructing a group:

1. Use some of the methods used for the instructional lesson.

2. Point to a word randomly. Going in seating order, the individual student says the word. Repeat with next student and so forth. Challenge each student to say the words as quickly as possible.

3. Point and randomly call a student's name. Student says the word quickly. Make this fast and be sure to call each student's name at least once.

4. Point to the words randomly and call an individual student's name, who then says the word as quickly as possible. It's OK to call on a student twice to keep all paying attention. Be sure everyone gets at least one turn. Select a word for an individual student; make it challenging or an easily named word.

5. The list of words is numbered. Point to the words randomly, saying the words with the students. Ask one student to give a sentence using one of the words. Other students raise their hand when they know which word was used. Student who gave the sentence should call on someone for the answer. After the word

is correctly named, circle the word used and have the student who named the word say a new sentence using one of the uncircled words, then call on someone else to tell which number was used. Circle the number. Repeat until all the words are used.

If instructing an individual:

1. Use some of the methods used for the instructional lesson.
2. Point to the words randomly; the student says the words as quickly as possible.
3. The list of words is numbered. Point to the words randomly; student and instructor say the words. Have the student give a sentence using one of the words. The instructor says the word in the list that was used by the student, circles the number in front of the word, and then gives a sentence using another word in the list. The student names the word used and circles the number in front of the word. Continue until the words have all been used.

Sight Word Evaluation and Instruction

Following directions in General Procedures for Reviewing Sight Words on pages 37 to 38, review the more difficult letter sounds and sight words that were previously taught.

Write the following new words on a list or on cards. Check each student individually. Allow the student five seconds to say each word. Record the responses for future use. With the student count how many words he/she already knows. Tell the student you will help him/her learn the words hc/shc didn't know.

was	they	have	are	I	from
there	one	word	what	were	your

If the student doesn't have instant recall, provide activities (see pages 14-16 and 29-30) to help with memorization and review of letter sounds and sight words previously taught. While doing this, also go to Section 9.

If the student has instant recall of the above words, go to Sections 9 and 10.

Phonics Evaluation: Consonants With More Than One Sound

Evaluate the student's ability to say the following consonant sounds and rules for why they make the sounds. These single consonants have more than one sound:

C c, G g, N n, Q q, S s, W w, X x, Y y

Instructor Background

The rules and sounds are listed below.

- *Cc* as in <u>c</u>ity

  The consonant *Cc* immediately followed by an *e, i,* or *y,* usually has its soft *Ss* sound as in <u>c</u>enter and <u>c</u>ycle.

- *Cc* as in <u>c</u>ake

  The consonant *Cc* <u>not</u> immediately followed by an *e, i,* or *y,* usually has the sound of *Kk* as in <u>c</u>at and cy<u>c</u>le.

- *Gg* as in <u>g</u>em

  The consonant *Gg* immediately followed by an *e, i,* or *y,* often has the sound of *Jj* as in <u>g</u>iraffe and <u>g</u>ypsy.

- *Gg* as in <u>g</u>oat

  The consonant *Gg* <u>not</u> immediately followed by an *e, i,* or *y,* often has its own hard sound as in <u>g</u>ate and <u>g</u>rass.

- *Nn* as in <u>n</u>ose

  The consonant *Nn* usually has its own sound as in <u>n</u>o and <u>n</u>est.

- *n* as in sa<u>ng</u>

  The consonant *n* immediately followed by *g*, often sounds like *n* and *g* are beginning to swallow their sounds as in si<u>ng</u> and sti<u>ng</u>.

- *n* as in si<u>nk</u>

  The consonant *n* immediately followed by *k*, usually sounds like *n* is beginning to swallow its sound, while *k* has its own sound as in ta<u>nk</u> and ri<u>nk</u>.

- *Qq* as in <u>qu</u>ick

  The consonant *Qq* has no sound of its own. *Qq* must have the vowel *u* immediately after it. Then *qu* has the sound of *k* and *w* together as in <u>qu</u>iet and <u>qu</u>ill.

- *Ss* as in <u>s</u>at

  The consonant *Ss* usually has its own soft sound as in <u>s</u>oft and <u>s</u>oup.

- *Ss* as in <u>su</u>re

  The consonant *Ss* immediately followed by the letter *u*, sometimes has the sound of *sh* as in <u>su</u>re and <u>su</u>gar.

- *s* as in no<u>se</u>

  The consonant *s* at the end of a word, immediately followed by an *e*, often has the sound of *z* as in clo<u>se</u> and ro<u>se</u>.

- *Ww* as in <u>w</u>et

  Ww is a consonant when it's at the beginning of a word. Then it usually has its own sound as in <u>w</u>in and <u>w</u>ish.

- *w* as in sa<u>w</u>

  w is a vowel when it immediately follows the vowels *a, e,* or *o.* Then the *w* combines with the vowel *a, e,* or *o* and has a new vowel sound as in s<u>aw</u>, n<u>ew</u> and sn<u>ow</u>.

- *x* as in bo<u>x</u>

  The consonant *x* at the inside or end of a word, usually has the sound of the letters *k* and *s* together as in si<u>x</u> and a<u>x</u>le.

- *Xx* as in <u>x</u>ylophone

  The consonant *x* at the beginning of a word has the sound of *z* as in <u>x</u>enon and <u>x</u>ylophone.

- *Yy* as in <u>y</u>es

  Yy is a always a consonant when it's at the beginning of a word and usually has its own sound as in <u>y</u>ellow and <u>y</u>et.

- *y* as in pl<u>ay</u>

  y is a vowel when the letters *ay* are together. Then *ay* has the long sound of *a* as in s<u>ay</u> and m<u>ay</u>.

- *y* as in cr<u>y</u>

  y is a vowel when it's at the end of a short one-syllable word. Then *y* usually has the long *i* vowel sound as in m<u>y</u> and fr<u>y</u>.

- *y* as in pupp<u>y</u>

  y is a vowel when it's at the end of a longer word with two or more syllables. Then *y* usually has the long *e* vowel sound as in bab<u>y</u> and funn<u>y</u>.

Procedures

Have the student tell you the sounds each letter makes and the basic rule for the consonant to make those sounds. The student may state the rules in his/her own words.

1. From an alphabet set, take the upper and lower case alphabet letters:

   Cc, Gg, Nn, Qq, Ss, Ww, Xx, Yy

2. Spread the letters randomly on the table or floor.

3. Ask the student to pick up a letter and say the different sounds it makes. With each sound, ask the student why it makes that sound. Sometimes there is a rule or reason for the sound and sometimes there isn't.

4. Put the letters for which all the sounds were said correctly in a pile.

5. Record the results so you know which sounds and rules to teach.

6. Together, count how many the student already knows. Tell the student you are surprised he knows some because most don't know very many of them and that you will help him/her learn the others.

If instructing a group: Since most students do not know all the above sounds or the rules that go with the consonants above, go to Section 10 with *all* students in a group. For some students it is good review; it teaches new knowledge to most students, and all students enjoy the stories. After Section 10, even students who previously knew many or most of the sounds and rules remember them and apply them better when figuring out (decoding) new words.

If instructing an individual: If the student knows none, some or many of the sounds and rules, go to Section 10. Review the sounds and rules the student did know and teach the ones not known. If the student knows all the sounds and rules with excellence, go to Section 11, page 67.

Phonics Instruction: Consonants With More Than One Sound

This section will take approximately one week to complete.

Sight Word and Letter Sound Review

Following directions in General Procedures for Reviewing Sight Words on pages 45 to 46, review any difficult letter sounds and sight words previously taught. Do this as many days during the week as needed.

Instructor Background

You will be using Silly Stories to help the students learn. Even older students chuckle at the stories. Elaborate on the stories making them your own. Enjoy the stories along with your students; draw illustrations while you tell the stories or copy the ones provided. After you have used a few stories, the students will possibly want to help tell a Silly Story. Be sure the story is true to the rules.

The sample words in each lesson are to help the students see how the rules work. Some of these words the students may know, most they will not know. These words do not need to be memorized at this time.

Procedures for Day One

1. Tell the Silly Story about *C*. As you tell it, draw the numbered pictures on a blank overhead transparency as the students watch.

Silly Story

The letter C had no sound of its own, poor C. C was so sad and tried so hard to make a sound of its own. (1) Then C remembered a story Momma Cat had read. It was about a cat who copied the sounds of other animals. Here is the story. "First Copy Cat copied the sound of a rooster, then a pig, a horse, and a mule. Next he walked into the forest and copied the sound of a bird and a squirrel."

Letter C thought, Mmmmm...maybe I could be a Copy Cat and copy other letter sounds. (2) I'll ask my best friends, S and K if I can copy their sounds." (3) Sure enough! Both S and K wanted to share their sounds. S said that whenever C had an E, I, or Y following it, C could copy its soft sound... ssss (as in the word soft.) K thought that was a good idea, so he said C could also copy its sound if an E, I, or Y <u>didn't</u> follow C. (4) C gave S and K a big smile, a big thank you and a big hug. C was a happy Copy Cat. K and S were happy they could help C.

2. Display the following sample words, which you have already written on an overhead transparency. These words are for students to *discover how the rule works*. The student is *not expected to memorize them*:

> came, call, come, circus, bicycle, place, color, car,
> cut, second, school, nice, can, could, cry

3. Guide the students to find if Copy Cat *C* followed the rules *S* and *K* gave. Write each word in the section by either *K* or *S* to show the sound Copy Cat used.

   • The consonant *C* immediately followed by an *E, I or Y*, usually has its soft *S* sound as in c<u>e</u>nter and c<u>y</u>cle.

   • The consonant *C* <u>not</u> immediately followed by an *E, I or Y*, usually has the sound of *K* as in <u>ca</u>t and cy<u>cl</u>e.

4. Use a follow-up activity. Have the students color a big *C* like you did, then put on ears, face and whiskers to turn it into Copy Cat *C*. Have the students put a *K* in the top right hand fourth of the paper, and an *S* in the bottom left hand fourth of the paper. Put *E, I* and *Y* after the *S*. Have them write the sample words in the corner with the *S* or *K*, to show which sound the *C* made in the word.

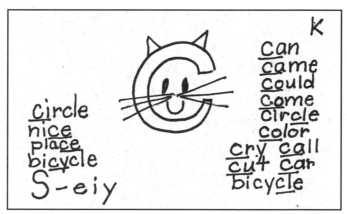

Procedures for Day Two

1. Tell the introductory Silly Story.

Silly Story

The letters G, N, S, W, and Y each have their own sounds, but sometimes they think just one sound is rather boring. They wanted to have a second sound also. So they often got together with other letter pals to do unusual, creative, and interesting things. Let's hear their silly stories.

2. Tell the Silly Story about *G*.

Silly Story

The letter G liked the plan that S and K had to help C. G had always admired the sound of J, so G asked J if he could copy the same idea. G explained the plan. If G had an e, i, or y following it, J would let G make its J sound. J agreed to the plan, but only if G would make its own hard sound when other letters were following it. G happily agreed. But I'll tell you a secret! The plan doesn't always work for G. I wonder why?

3. Display the following sample words, which you have already written on an overhead transparency. These words are for students to *discover how the rule works*. The student is *not expected to memorize them*.

    page, green, good, large, great, gave, give, girl, grow, get

4. Guide the students to find if *G* follows the rules *J* gave it. Tell the students, *"Sometimes the plan works for G and sometimes it doesn't. I don't know why? Do you?"*

    • The consonant *G* immediately followed by an *E, I, or Y*, often has the sound of *J* as in <u>gi</u>raffe and <u>gy</u>psy.

    • The consonant *G* <u>not</u> immediately followed by an *E, I, or Y*, often has its own hard sound as in <u>ga</u>te and <u>gr</u>ass.

5. Follow-up activity. Have the students make a big *G* in the middle of a paper. Have the students make a *J* in the upper right hand fourth of the paper. Have them write the sample words on the *J* fourth of the paper if *G* used the *J* sound. Underneath the *G*, have them write the words with the *G* sound.

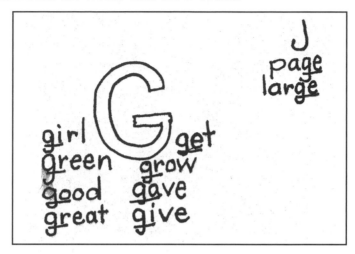

6. Tell the following Silly Story about *N*.

Silly Story

Another unusual thing about G…some of the time when G follows N, they are both so shy, it sounds like N and G are both beginning to swallow their sounds. Listen carefully to hear N and G beginning to swallow their sounds. Listen… sing. Now say the word sing. "Sing"

But let me tell you, K sure isn't shy when it follows N. K just goes right ahead and says its own sound while shy N still begins to swallow its sound. Listen carefully to hear N begin to swallow its sound while K blurts out its sound. Listen…think. Now say the word think. "Think."

7. Display these sample words, which you have already written on an overhead transparency. These words are for students to *discover how the rule works*. The student is *not expected to memorize them*.

in, no, run, and, hand, sing, ring, hang,
song, long, rung, ink, think

8. Guide the students to find if *N* does what the Silly Story said.

- The consonant *N* usually has its own sound as in <u>n</u>o and <u>n</u>est.

- The consonant *N* immediately followed by *G*, often sounds like *N* and *G* are beginning to swallow their sounds as in si<u>ng</u> and sti<u>ng</u>.

- The consonant *N* immediately followed by *K*, usually sounds like *N* is beginning to swallow its sound, while *K* has its own sound as in ta<u>nk</u> and ri<u>nk</u>.

9. Follow-up activity. Use the *G* picture the students made. In the bottom left hand fourth of the paper have them make an *N*. In the upper left hand fourth of the paper, have them write *NG*. Put heads on the *N* and *G* with smile lines to show shy down-looking eyes. Give them legs with feet turning in to show shyness. Put *NK* in the lower right hand fourth of the paper. Put head and legs on the *NK*. Put a face with a smile line to show shy down-eyes, and turned in feet on *N*. Put a circle mouth on *K* to show its boldly saying its sound. Have the students write the sample words with *N, NG,* or *NK* to show the sound made in each word.

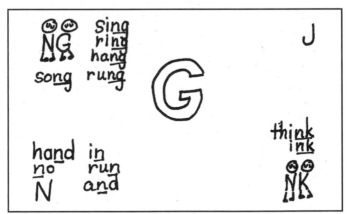

Procedures for Day Three

1. Tell the Silly Story about *S*.

Silly Story

S liked its own sound. It sounded like a snake's sound sss, but S had a problem. When it was at the end of a word, E sometimes tagged right behind him, begging S to make the sound of Z—zzz. S finally asked Z for permission to make the Z sound when E tagged along behind it. Z said, "OK, S use the Z sound when E tags along behind and begs to hear zzz, but only at the end of a word." That solved Ss problem with E.

When U found out that S got permission to make the sound of Z when e tagged along, U thought, "Mmmmm... maybe S can sometimes make my favorite sound, too...SH." So U asked S if it could make the SH sound when it tagged along. "Sure," said S, "but only some of the time. "And I just made the SH sound!"

2. Display these sample words, which you have already written on an overhead transparency. These words are for students to *discover how the rule works*. The student is *not expected to memorize them.*

    so, this, is, just, nose, sit, rose, sure, sugar

3. Guide the students to find if *S* does what the Silly Story said. Sometimes it is difficult to hear the *Z* sound, but you can do it if you listen carefully.

    • The consonant *S* usually has its own soft sound as in <u>s</u>oft and <u>s</u>oup.

    • The consonant *S* immediately followed by the letter *u*, sometimes has the sound of *SH* as in <u>su</u>re and <u>su</u>gar.

    • The consonant *S* at the end of a word, immediately followed by an *E*, often has the sound of *Z* as in clo<u>se</u> and ro<u>se</u>.

4. Follow-up activity. Have the students make a big *S* in the middle of a paper. Put *SH* in the upper right hand fourth of the paper. Put

Z in the top left hand fourth of the paper. Have the students write the sample words that have the *S* sound under the *S* and the words that have the *Z* or *SH* sound on the paper with those letters.

Procedures for Day Four

1. Tell the Silly Story about *Ww*.

Silly Story

W liked making its own sound and usually did it when it was the first letter in a word. However, being rather musical, W liked hearing different sounds.

One day W noticed that the vowel letters A, E, and O often walked in front of it. W thought it would be fun if A, E, and O made some new sounds along with it. After discussing it together A, E, and O said when one of them walked in front of W they would make a new sound with W.

So when W saw A, E, or O in front of it, the two of them made new sounds like AW as in s<u>aw</u>, EW as in n<u>ew</u>, OW as in h<u>ow</u>, and OW as in sh<u>ow</u>. The sounds were musical to W.

2. Display these sample words, which you have already written on an overhead transparency. These words are for students to *discover how the rule works*. The student is *not expected to memorize them*.

saw, new, how, win, few, cow, grow, law, wish

3. Guide the students to find the different sounds W makes and to notice the different sounds it makes with *A, E,* and *O.*

   • *W* is a consonant when it's at the beginning of a word. Then it usually has its own sound as in <u>w</u>in and <u>w</u>ish.

   • W is a vowel when it immediately follows the vowels *A, E,* or *O.* Then the *W* combines with the vowel *A, E,* or *O* and has a new vowel sound as in s<u>aw</u>, n<u>ew</u>, h<u>ow</u> and sn<u>ow</u>.

4. Follow-up activity. Make a picture with *W* in the middle of the paper. Put *AW* in one corner, *EW* in one corner and *OW* in one corner. Write the words that have the *W* sound under the *W.* Write the other words with the letters that make the right sound.

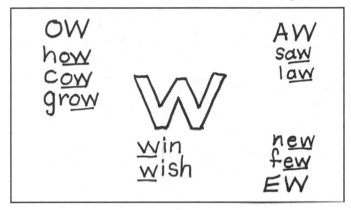

1. Tell the Silly Story about *Y.*

Silly Story

Y loved being at the beginning and the ending of words. Y made its own sound at the beginning of words like in its favorite color yellow, but it was very difficult to make that sound at the end of words. I and E decided to give Y a wonderful gift.

Since I got lonely at the end of a short word, I said Y could take its place and make I's long sound. E said Y could take its place at the end of a longer word and make E's long sound. Y loved the gift so much, it gave E and I a hug. A was feeling left out, so Y told A it could be in front of it sometimes, and the Y would take a rest and let A sing out its own long A sound. A gave Y a hug.

2. Display these sample words, which you have already written on an overhead transparency. These words are for students to *discover how the rule works*. The student is *not expected to memorize them*.

> you, yellow, funny, cry, baby, may, my, play

3. Guide the students to find if *A* and *Y* were in places that made each of them happy. Notice the sounds *Y* makes.

  • *Y* is a always a consonant when it's at the beginning of a word and usually has its own sound as in y̲ellow and y̲et.

  • *Y* is a vowel when the letters *AY* are together. Then *AY* has the long sound of *A* as in sa̲y̲ and ma̲y̲.

  • *Y* is a vowel when it's at the end of a short one-syllable word. Then *Y* usually has the long *I* vowel sound as in my̲ and fry̲.

  • *Y* is a vowel when it's at the end of a longer word with two or more syllables. Then *Y* usually has the long *E* vowel sound as in bab̲y̲ and funny̲.

4. Follow-up activity. Have the students make a big *Y* in the middle of a paper. Put an *E* in the top right fourth of the paper. Put the letter *A* in the bottom right fourth of the paper and an *I* in the top left fourth of the paper. Write the words that made the *Y*s consonant sound under the *Y*. Write the other words with the letter whose name *Y* said.

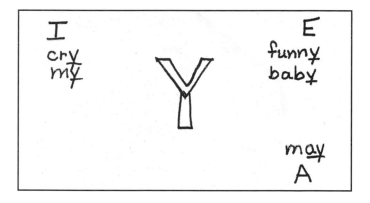

Procedures for Day Five

1. Tell the Silly Story about *X* and *Q*.

Silly Story

Just like Copy Cat C, the letters X and Q had <u>no</u> sound of their own. After they saw that K and S helped Copy Cat C, they too tried to get some help. They found K, S, W, and Z fishing off the dock. After X and Q fished with K, S, W, and Z for a while, they told them they needed to have help making a sound. All the letters wanted to help.

Z said it didn't get to use its sound much and would X like to use its sound whenever X was at the beginning of a word? "Yes, yes," said happy X, making its new sound Z, Z, Z.

K and S said X could copy their sounds, too, if X smooshed them together to make its new sound. X tried it: "KS, KS." X liked the new sound of KS. No other letter had a sound like that! X danced around singing its new sound over and over: "KS, KS, KS."

---

2. Display these sample words, which you have already written on an overhead transparency. These words are for students to *discover how the rule works*. The student is *not expected to memorize them*.

   box, fox, ax, fax, sax, mix, wax, xylophone

3. Guide the students to find the *X* in the words and to duplicate its sound, which copies the letters *KS*.

   •The consonant *X* at the inside or end of a word, usually has the sound of the letters *K* and *S* together as in si<u>x</u> and a<u>x</u>le.

   •The consonant *X* at the beginning of a word has the sound of *Z* as in <u>x</u>enon and <u>x</u>ylophone.

4. Tell the rest of the Silly Story about Q.

Silly Story

Now it was time to help Q. K really liked the smooshed sound of KS that X got, so K told W that smooshed together <u>they</u> would make a nice KW sound for Q. They knew that Q was forgetful, so they asked the letter U to follow Q in every word, helping Q remember its new smooshed sound of KW. And that's why you always find the letter U following the letter Q and why Q always remembers its smooshed sound, KW, KW, KW.

5. Display these sample words, which you have already written on an overhead transparency. These words are for students to *discover how the rule works*. The student is *not expected to memorize them*.

    quick, quack, quiet, square, queen, quit

6. Guide the students to find *QU* in the words and duplicate the sound, which copies the letters *KW*.

    • The consonant *Qq* has no sound of its own. *Qq* must have the vowel *U* immediately after it. Then *QU* has the sound of *K* and *W* together as in <u>qu</u>iet and <u>qu</u>ill.

7. Follow-up activities. Have the students fold a paper in half. Put a big *X* on one half of the paper and *Q* on the other side. Put an underlined *KS* with the *X* and an underlined *KW* with the *Q*. Write the sample words on the correct half of the paper.

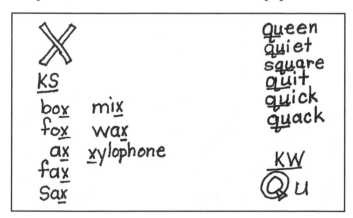

If the students know the sounds and understand the rules in Section 10 reasonably well, go on to Section 11. The rules and words in this lesson will be repeated in future lessons.

Sight Word Evaluation and Instruction

Evaluate and teach the following set of sight words. These words should be memorized.

do	each	their	said	many	some
two	other	would	about	out	look

If the students can't say these words instantly, teach them using repetition and interesting activities. Also review sounds and sight words previously taught that need reteaching. When the students can say most words in Section 11, go to Section 12.

If instructing a group: If a student can instantly recall the above words, go on to Section 13. Give this student Section 12 with the rest of the class, when it is taught.

If instructing an individual: Go to Sections 12 and 13.

Phonics Instruction: Two Consonants That Make One Sound

All students should receive the instruction from this section. It teaches new knowledge to most students and is good review for others. This section will take one week to complete.

Sight Word and Letter Sound Review

Following directions in General Procedures for Reviewing Sight Words on pages 45 to 46, review any difficult letter sounds and sight words previously taught. Do this as many days during the week as needed.

Instructor Background

Sometimes when two consonant letters are together, they make one sound, such as *SH, CH, CK* and *PH*. Their sounds do not use the voice box, but have an unvoiced sound. When the two letters *TH* and the two letters *WH* are together, they also make an unvoiced sound; in addition, they sometimes use the voice box to make a voiced sound.

Once again you will be using Silly Stories to help the students learn. The sample words in each lesson are to help the students *see how the rules work*. Some of these words the students may know; most they will not know. These words do *not need to be memorized at this time*.

Procedures for Day One

1. Explain to the students they will be learning about two consonant letters together that have one sound. Tell the students the two letters may make a sound using the voice box. The two letters maybe won't make a sound using the voice box, or they may even use the voice box sometimes and not other times. Tell the students the letters they'll be learning about during the week are *TH, WH, CH, SH, CK,* and *PH.*

2. Display the big letters *TH* and these sample words, which you have already written on the transparency. These words are for students to *discover how the rule works*. Even though students will have memorized some of these, they are *not expected to memorize all of them now*.

> the, then, that, than, they, think, with,
> mother, father, there, other, thought

3. Read the words to the students. Have them repeat each word after you.

4. Have the students perform an experiment to find in which words the *TH* uses the voice box and in which words the *TH* does not use the voice box. Follow these steps.

   a. Ask the students to hold a hand very close to their mouth. Say the first word together…*the*.

   b. Ask the students to gently place a hand over their throat. Say the first word together…*the*.

   c. Ask the students if the *TH* blew air out and did not make their voice box vibrate. No.

   d. Ask the students if the *TH* made their voice box vibrate and did not blow air out. Yes.

   e. Check the students' decisions by reading the word again and noticing if the air blew out or if the voice box vibrated.

5. With each word repeat the steps in number 4. Write the words that use a voiced sound (the voice box) in one list and the words that used no voice sound (unvoiced) in a second list.

6. Tell the Silly Story about *TH* and *WH.*

Silly Story

TH and WH sometimes got laryngitis. (You know what that is—when your voice doesn't make any sound, but your mouth still says it with air.)

Well, TH could get laryngitis a lot when it was at the end of a word, but TH could have it happen to it when it was any place at all in a word. When it didn't have laryngitis it used its voice.

WH got laryngitis most of the time at the beginning of a word. It, too, used its voice whenever it didn't have laryngitis.

7. Go over the words to find how well *TH* followed the rules.
   Voiced...the, then, that, than, they, mother, father, there, other
   Unvoiced...think, with, thought

   • The consonants *TH* may have an unvoiced or voiced sound when they are at the beginning or the middle or the end of a word as in <u>th</u>ought and mo<u>th</u>er.

   • The consonants *TH* usually have an unvoiced sound when they are at the end of a word as in wi<u>th</u>.

Procedures for Day Two

1. Tell students they'll be working with the letters *WH* when they are together.

2. Display the big letters *WH* and these sample words, which you have already written on the transparency. These words are for students to *discover how the rule works*. The students are *not expected to memorize all of them now*.

   what, why, who, when, where, which

3. Read the words to the students. Have them repeat each word after you.

4. Have the students check to see in which words *WH* uses a voice box or does not use a voice box. Follow these steps again.

   a. Ask the students to hold a hand very closely to their mouth. Say the first word together…*what.*

   b. Ask the students to gently place a hand over their throat. Say the first word together…*what.*

   c. Ask the students if the *WH* blew air out and did not make their voice box vibrate. Yes.

   d. Ask the students if the *WH* made their voice box vibrate and did not blow air out. No.

   e. Check the students' decisions by reading the word again and noticing if the air blew out or if their voice box vibrated.

5. With each word repeat the steps in number 4. Write the words that use a voiced sound (the voice box) in one list and the words that used no voice sound (unvoiced) in a second list.

6. Ask the students to recall the Silly Story about *TH* and *WH.*

7. Go over the words to find out how well *WH* followed the rules.
Unvoiced…what, why, when, where, which
Voiced…who

8. Make a big question mark around the words on the transparency. Ask the students why they think you did that. Help them detect that each of the words can begin a question.

   •The letters *WH* usually have an unvoiced sound and are usually at the beginning of a word as in <u>wh</u>ale, <u>wh</u>ip, <u>wh</u>eel, <u>wh</u>ite

   • The letters *WH* may have an voiced sound as in <u>wh</u>o.

Procedures for Day Three

1. Explain to the students they will be learning about the letters *CH* and *SH*. They are both formed the same way and both use no voice box. However, one is quieter than the other.

2. Display the big letters *CH* and *SH*.

3. Tell the Silly Story about *CH* and *SH*.

Silly Story

The letters SH and CH noticed how confused TH and WH were with their rules, so they decided to make simpler rules for themselves. Both SH and CH had laryngitis, so they had to find sounds that didn't use voices.

CH, who loved trains, decided it would use a loud sound like the steam engine of a train saying ch–ch–ch–ch.

SH chose to use a quieter sound, like sh–sh–sh. Now SH tiptoes around so quietly, as if someone is sleeping, saying sh–sh–sh–sh.

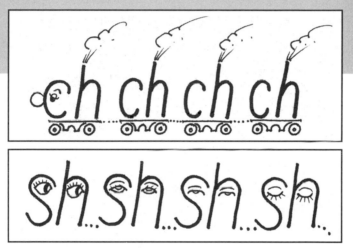

4. Tell the students to listen for the *SH* and *CH* sounds while you say each sample word. Have the students repeat each word after you, while listening for the *SH* or *CH* sound. These words are for students to *discover how the rule works*. They are *not expected to memorize them.*

   she, each, which, show, much, such, fish

5. Repeat the words again. Have the students repeat the word and tell you the sound they heard, *CH* or *SH*. Write the words under the *SH* or *CH* on the transparency.

6. Reread the words one at a time. Have the students check to see if the words are in the correct place.

- The consonants *CH* can be anywhere in a word and usually have the sound as in <u>ch</u>urch and ea<u>ch</u>.
- The consonants *SH* can be anywhere in a word and usually have the sound as in <u>sh</u>op and fi<u>sh</u>.

Procedures for Day Four

1. Explain to the students they will be learning about the letters *CK*.
2. Write the big letters *CK* on a transparency upon which you already wrote the sample words. These words are for students to *discover how the rule works*. They are *not expected to memorize them*.

   back, stick, pick, lock, pocket

3. Read the words. Have the students repeat the word after each one.
4. Ask them to see if they can figure out a rule for *CK*. Ask them what they figured out.
   - The consonants *CK* usually follow a single vowel that has a short sound and is in the middle or end of words.
   - *CK* usually has the sound of *K* as in ba<u>ck</u> and po<u>ck</u>et.
5. Tell the Silly Story about *CK*.

Silly Story

Since K was nice enough to let C copy its sound so often, C promised K that when they were together, it wouldn't copy Ks sound at all, and that K could do all the talking. So when we see CK go along together, we hear only K making its sound.

6. Read each word again. Have the students repeat. Check to see if the rule(s) they figured out worked.

Procedures for Day Five

1. Explain to the students they they will be learning about the letters *PH*.

2. Write the big letters *PH* on a transparency, on which you already wrote the sample words. These words are for students to *discover how the rule works*. They are *not expected to memorize them*.

phone, photo

3. Read the words. Have the students repeat the word after each one.

4. Ask them if they can figure out a rule for *PH*.

   • The consonants *PH* can be anywhere in a word and usually have the sound of *F* as in telephone and phrase.

5. Tell the Silly Story about *PH*.

Silly Story

P and H were only able to get together for a few words, so they wanted to make one of their favorite sounds when they were together. They both agreed F had their favorite sound. They just loved to hear Fs sound. Off they went to see if F would let them make its lovely sound. F overheard them talking and felt very honored that P and H wanted to use its sound. Of course, he let them use it. Whenever you see PH walking together, remember they make the sound of F.

When the letter sounds in Section 12 are learned by most students, go to Section 13, if it is not yet completed.

Sight Word Evaluation and Instruction

Evaluate and teach the following set of sight words:

number	long	come	who	oil	could
water	part	people	been	find	over
into	see	which	call		

If the students can't say the words above instantly, teach these words using repetition and interesting activities. Also review sounds and sight words previously taught that need reteaching.

If a student has completed Sections 1 through 11 before the majority of the group is ready to move on, provide him/her with books to read or listen to on cassettes. This will allow the student to develop new vocabulary using skills that have been learned, while experiencing the joy of reading.

Individually recheck each student on letters and sight vocabulary previously not known well. Keep notes on words and sounds that still need further review.

Send home a copy of Appendix C for students and parents to review together.

Play the Memory Game, then go on to Section 14.

Memory Game

Object of Game: To provide a fun way for giving students additional memorization practice on the basic sight words.

Players: Two to four players is the ideal number, but up to six can play if there are enough cards.

Supplies:
- Twelve to twenty-four cards using words that the students in the group need more practice memorizing
- Write the same word on two cards, making sets of two matching cards. A game with twelve cards will give the students practice with six words. Turn each card face down and put a symbol such as "/" on the top left corner. This / mark indicates that the word is right side up. It also helps the instructor identify that the words in this set of cards go with a specific lesson, such as Unit II, Section 13. Change the mark for each set of words.
- An oven timer

Setup: Players should sit at a table, where all can easily read the cards.

The Play: The first player turns over a card and says the word. If the other players say it's correct, he turns over a second card and says the word. If the words are a match, he takes both cards off the table, keeps them, and takes a second turn. If he does not get a match, both cards are turned over, staying in the same location on the table, and the next person takes a turn. Play continues.

Ending the Game: Play ends when all the cards have been matched. The winner has the most cards.

Variations: Change the word cards, adding new words that need to be practiced more. For example, if the students have problems with words that look similar, such as "where," "were," "there," "their," "when," "went," "want," "with," and "which," make a game using them.

Phonics Instruction: Short and Long Vowel Sounds

All students should receive the instruction as a group. Because this session takes more preparation than usual, read through all of Section 14, then secure and prepare the necessary materials. This section will take two weeks to complete.

Sight Word and Letter Sound Review

Follow directions in General Procedures for Reviewing Sight Words on pages 45 to 46, reviewing any difficult letter sounds and sight words previously taught.

Instructor Background

The vowels are *Aa, Ee, Ii, Oo,* and *Uu*. When the name of the vowel letter is said, no part of the mouth has to touch another part of the mouth for the letter to be a consonant. *Aa, Ee, Ii, Oo,* and *Uu* each have a long and short vowel sound. Some of the time *Yy* and *Ww* are vowels. The long vowel sounds are the easiest to learn, because the name of the vowel letter is the long sound of the vowel—*A, E, I, O,* and *U*. The short vowel sounds are usually harder for students to learn because each vowel takes a new sound. Knowing the vowel sounds helps readers figure out unknown words.

Long Vowel Sounds

The long vowel sound of each vowel sounds like its name.

> *Aa*   as in <u>a</u>pe and h<u>ay</u>
>
> *Ee*   as in s<u>ee</u> and l<u>ea</u>p

> *Ii*   as in l<u>i</u>ke and ch<u>i</u>ld
> *Oo*   as in h<u>o</u>pe and s<u>oa</u>p
> *Uu*   as in <u>u</u>se and bl<u>ue</u>

Short Vowel Sounds

The short vowel sounds each have a new sound. (Also see the short vowel sounds chart on pages 73 to 74.)

> *Aa*   as in fl<u>a</u>t and <u>a</u>pple
> *Ee*   as in m<u>e</u>t and <u>e</u>gg
> *Ii*   as in s<u>i</u>t and <u>i</u>gloo
> *Oo*   as in l<u>o</u>t and <u>o</u>ctopus
> *Uu*   as in c<u>u</u>p and <u>u</u>mbrella

Procedures for Day One

1. Ask the students to name the letters while you write them on a blank transparency—*A, E, I, O,* and *U.* Use the term name as often as possible. Tell them these letters are each vowels. Have the students name the vowels again.

2. Point to each vowel in order and have the students name it. Point to each vowel, but this time not in any order and have the students name the vowels.

3. Tell the students each vowel has a long and a short sound. Tell them you understand they already know each vowel's long sound because they said it every time you pointed to a vowel. Ask them to say the vowel's long sound again as you point to it.

4. Cover the letters and ask if anyone can name all the vowels. Be surprised when many raise their hands.

5. Uncover the vowel letters. Check with the students. Ask if anyone can give all the vowels long sounds. Once again, act surprised when many raise their hands. Ask everyone who knows to name the long vowel sounds as you point to them out of order.

6. Follow-up activity. Cut vowel letters from magazines and newspapers for a given period of time…ten, fifteen, or twenty minutes. Then have each make a collage of the vowel letters by pasting them on a piece of colored paper.

Short Vowel Chart

VOWEL	SOUND	OBJECT	PICTURE
A	a	Apple with oval shape, like a delicious apple, with leaves on the stem. It can be real or imitation. After the lesson, put the apple in the Vowel Display.	
E	e	Egg, decorated like it might be for Easter. I like to use a sugar decorated egg. After the lesson, put the egg in the Vowel Display.	
I	i	Igloo, made of sugar cubes or both sizes of marshmallows. After the lesson, put the igloo in the Vowel Display.	
O	o	A plain doughnut with a hole in the middle. I set mine out to harden in the air for a week ahead of the lesson. After the lesson, put the doughnut in the Vowel Display.	
U	u	An umbrella with a crook for the handle, even if you have to make a crook on the umbrella. After the lesson, put the umbrella in the Vowel Display.	

ACTIVITIES

A Give each child a red delicious apple. Tell them they will be eaten later, to look at the shape now. Is it more like a circle, square, triangle, rectangle or oval? Make a printed a with a heavy black marker. With a red marker trace the oval of the a. Add leaves with green. Ask them what you turned the a into. Have them say apple, then get stuck on the first sound and say the short sound of A -- a, a, a, a. Allow them to eat the apple. For an art project, have them make an a with black paint marker, then paint the apple red, and add leaves.

E Show a decorated egg. Ask them to look at the shape. Is it more like a circle, square, triangle or oval? Make a printed e, oval shaped, with a heavy black marker. With colored markers decorate the e to look like a decorated egg. Have them say egg, then get stuck on the first sound and say the short sound of E -- e, e, e, e. For an art project, using a black crayon, have each make a large e on a piece of colored construction paper. Decorate the e. Provide them with an egg snack.

I Show the igloo and ask what it is. Where might people make an igloo? (Answer: In the Arctic and Antarctic areas, where snow is more plentiful than any other material.) Have them say igloo, then get stuck on the first sound and say the short sound of I -- i, i, i, i. For an art project, provide each student with marshmallows and/or sugar cubes so each can make an igloo. If so desired, the marshmallows and sugar cubes can first be used for a math lesson. Give some marshmallows to them for snacks!

O Show the small doughnut and ask what shape it is most like -- a square, rectangle, circle or oval. Draw the doughnut shape with a black marker. Ask what letter shape it is like. Draw a pan under the doughnut with lines indicating heat going up from the pan. Tell a Silly Story: A little round as an O doughnut watched while the other doughnuts were put into hot grease. They looked so nice when they came out, but he was afraid. Finally it was his turn. It was so hot! He didn't have to stay there for very long, though. When he came out of the hot grease it felt so good he said, "Ah" -- the short sound of the letter O, his shape. Have the students make the sound the O doughnut made when he came out of the hot grease, the short o sound -- ah, ah, ah, ah. Give each student a small doughnut to eat. Using a black marker, have each student draw a big round O with a smaller O inside of it. Color the doughnut. For an additional project, make and fry doughnuts together or go to a bakery and watch them make doughnuts.

U Show the umbrella with a crook in the handle. Ask what vowel letter shape the handle reminds them of. Yes, the letter U. Draw the letter U with a black marker and color inside the U. Open the umbrella and ask them what the whole object is. Yes, an umbrella. Make a stem going up from the right side of the U, and draw the opened umbrella over the U. Have them say the word umbrella, but get stuck on the first sound, the short sound of U -- u, u, u, u. For an art project, have each draw a u with black marker and color inside it. Paste a strip of paper for the stem of the umbrella and then cut the top of the umbrella shape from wrapping paper. Paste it on the stem.

Procedures for Day Two

1. Explain to the students they will be learning the short vowel sounds during the week, and today they will learn the short *A* vowel sound.

2. Give the students a red apple. Tell them it can be eaten later but to look at the shape now. Ask if it is more like a circle, square, triangle, rectangle, or oval? Likely, it will look oval.

3. With a black transparency marker, draw a large oval. With a red transparency marker, trace around the black oval, making a lower case manuscript letter a. Put a dip in the top like an apple has and a little dip in the bottom like an apple has. See the Short Vowel Chart.

4. Ask, "What letter did the red marker make?" *A*. With a green marker add a stem and leaves. Ask, "What fruit was drawn?" Apple. Tell the students the apple is to help them remember the short a vowel sound.

5. Have the students say "apple" again. Then again, but get stuck on the first sound, repeating it over and over. With the students, say *A—A—A—A—A*. Tell them they just made the short sound of the vowel *A*.

6. Have the students get stuck on the first sound in apple again, the short *A* vowel sound. Write on the transparency as the short *A* vowel sound is made, *A—A—A—A—A*. Then put a smile over each *A* while you tell the students you are making the symbol for a short *A* sound.

7. Follow-up activity. For an art project, have the students make an big oval with a black crayon or marker, then with a red crayon or marker trace around the black oval, making a lower case manuscript letter *A*. Put a dip in the top like an apple has and a little dip in the bottom like an apple has. With a green marker add a stem and leaves. Put a smile above the apple to help them remember the short vowel sound of *A*. Allow the students to eat the apple.

Procedures for Day Three

1. Hold up an artificial apple, ask the students of what vowel letter the apple reminds them. *A*. Have them make the short vowel sound, *A—A—A—A*, while you write the *A* with a smile over it on

a transparency. Place the artificial apple in a display area labeled "short vowel sounds."

2. Show the students a decorated egg, similar to an Easter egg. Ask the students to look at the shape. Ask if it is more like a circle, square, triangle, rectangle, or oval. *Oval.*

3. With a black transparency marker, draw a large oval. With a colored transparency marker, trace a lower case manuscript e around the black oval, leaving some of the right hand side open but add the line through the middle. See the Short Vowel Chart.

4. Ask, "What letter did the colored marker make?" *E.* With other colored markers simply decorate the *E* to look like a decorated egg. Ask, "What was drawn?" *Decorated egg.* Tell the students the egg is to help them remember the short *E* vowel sound.

5. Have the students say egg. Then say it again, but get stuck on the first sound and repeat it over and over. With the students say, *E—E—E—E—E.* Tell the students they just made the short sound of the vowel *E.*

6. Have the students get stuck on the first sound in egg again, the short *E* vowel sound. Write on the transparency as the short *E* vowel sound is made, *E—E—E—E—E.* Then put a smile over each *E* while you tell the students you are making the symbol for a short *E* sound.

7. Follow-up activity. For an art project, have the students make an big oval with a black crayon or marker, then with a colored crayon or marker trace around the black oval, making a lower case manuscript letter *E* leaving some of the right hand side open, and putting a line through the middle. With other colored markers have the students simply decorate the *E* to look like a decorated egg. Ask them to put a smile above the egg to help them remember the short vowel sound of *E.*

Procedures for Day Four

1. Hold up the decorated egg. Ask the students of what vowel letter the egg reminds them. *E.* Have them make the short vowel sound, *E—E—E—E,* while you write the *E* with a smile over it on the overhead transparency. Hold up the artificial apple. Ask them of what short vowel sound the apple reminds them. Repeat

it. *A—A—A—A*. Place the decorated egg and the apple in the display area labeled "short vowel sounds."

2. On the transparency draw a big picture of an igloo with a big door. Ask the students what it is and in what part of the world people might make an igloo. In the arctic where snow is more plentiful than any other material. See the Short Vowel Chart.

3. Ask the students to say igloo, then to get stuck on the first sound and repeat, *I—I—I—I*. With a black marker, draw a lower case letter *I* in the igloo doorway. Put a circle above it for the dot. Ask, "What letter was drawn in the doorway?" *I*. Tell the students they have been saying the short vowel sound for the letter *I*.

4. With a blue marker, turn the *I* into a person with arms and hands close to the side. Put a belt on the person and tell them that when the belt buckle is pushed, the person says the short *I* sound. What is the short *I* sound? Have them push their imaginary belt buckle and say *I—I—I—I*. Put a smile above the *I* person as they say the short sound.

5. Have them say igloo and get stuck again, *I—I—I—I*. Put the short vowel symbol over the *I* as it is said. Tell the students the igloo and the person are to help them remember the short *I* vowel sound.

6. Follow-up activity. For an art project, with a black marker, have the students draw a big igloo with a big door. With a black marker or crayon, put a lower case *I* with a circle dot above it, in the doorway. With a blue marker, turn the *I* into a person with arms and hands close to the side. Put a belt on the person. Ask them to put a smile above the *I* person to help them remember the short vowel sound of *I*. The students may also make an igloo from miniature marshmallows or sugar cubes.

Procedures for Day Five

1. Hold up an igloo made of marshmallows or sugar cubes, with a cardboard *I* person in the door. Ask the students of what vowel letter the igloo and person remind them. *I*. Have them make the short vowel sound, *I—I—I—I,* while you write the *I* with a smile over it on the overhead transparency.

2. Hold up the decorated egg. Ask them of what short vowel sound it reminds them of. *E*. Repeat its sound, *E—E—E—E,* while you write the *E* with a smile over it on the overhead transparency.

3. Hold up the artificial apple. Ask them of what short vowel sound the apple reminds them. Repeat its sound, *A—A—A—A,* while you write the *A* with a smile over it on the overhead transparency. Place the apple, the egg, and the igloo in the display area labeled "short vowel sounds."

4. Show the students a small doughnut. Ask them what shape it's most like—a square, rectangle, circle, or oval. Circle. Ask what vowel letter shape it is like. *O.* Draw the doughnut shape with a black marker. Make a big *O* with a smaller *O* inside it. Draw a pan under the doughnut shape with lines indicating heat is going up from the pan. See the Short Vowel Chart.

5. Tell a Silly Story.

Silly Story

A little O shaped doughnut watched while the other doughnuts were put into hot grease. They looked so nice when they came out. Finally it was little O's turn. Ouch, the grease was so hot! Little O didn't have to stay there long before it was taken out of the pan. When little O came out of the hot grease it felt so good it sighed, "Ah." From then on little O kept Ah as its short sound.

6. Ask the students to say the sound the little *o* doughnut sighed when it came out of the hot grease. *Ah, Ah, Ah, Ah.* Make a big smile above the *O* and on the *O.* Tell the students they've just made the short *O* vowel sound. Ask the students to repeat the short *O* vowel sound *O—O—O—O* while you put the smile above the *O*s. See the Short Vowel Chart.

7. Have them once again say what the little *o* doughnut said when he came out of the grease. *O—O—O—O.* Tell the students the doughnut is to help them remember the short *O* vowel sound.

8. Follow-up activity. With a black marker or crayon, have each student draw a big round *O* with a smaller *O* inside it. Put a pan under it with heat marks going up from it. Put a smile above and on the *O.* Give each student a small doughnut to eat. For an additional activity, make doughnuts reading the recipe and measuring the ingredients or go to a bakery and watch them make doughnuts.

Procedures for Day Six

1. Hold up a small doughnut. Ask the students of what vowel letter the doughnut reminds them. *O.* Have them make the short *O* vowel sound while you write on the transparency, *O—O—O—O* with a smile over them.

2. Hold up the igloo made of marshmallows or sugar cubes with a cardboard *I* person in the door. Ask the students of what vowel sound the igloo and person remind them. *I.* Repeat its short sound, *I—I—I—I.*

3. Hold up the decorated egg. Ask them of what vowel sound it reminds them. *E.* Repeat its short sound, *E—E—E—E.*

4. Hold up the artificial apple. Ask them of what short vowel sound the apple reminds them. *A.* Repeat it, *A—A—A—A.* Place the apple, egg, igloo, and doughnut in the display area labeled "short vowel sounds."

5. Open an umbrella so the curve of the handle resembles a *U.* Ask the students what vowel letter the shape of the handle reminds them of. *U.* Draw a big *U* on the transparency and a smaller *U* inside it. Leave room on the paper to add an umbrella above it. With a colored marker color inside the two *U*s so it now looks like a handle.

6. Make a stem going up the right side of the *U* and draw an opened umbrella over the *U.* Ask the students what you drew. Umbrella.

7. Have them say the word umbrella but get stuck on the first sound, *U—U—U—U.* Tell them they have said the short vowel sound of *U.* Ask them to repeat it, *U—U—U—U,* while you put the short symbol above the *U*s on the transparency. Tell them the umbrella is to remind them of the short *U* sound. Repeat the short *U* vowel sound again, *U—U—U—U.*

8. Follow-up activity. Have the students use a black marker to draw a big *U* with a smaller one inside it. Color inside the two *U*s. Cut and paste a strip of paper for the stem of the umbrella. Cut the top of the umbrella shape from wrapping paper. Paste the umbrella shape on the stem.

Procedures for Day Seven

1. Hold up the umbrella. Ask the students of what vowel letter the umbrella reminds them. *U*. Have them make the short *U* vowel sound while you write on the transparency, *U—U—U—U* with a smile over them.

2. Hold up a small doughnut. Ask the students of what vowel letter the doughnut reminds them. *O*. Repeat its short sound, *O—O—O—O*.

3. Hold up the igloo made of marshmallows or sugar cubes with a cardboard *I* person in the door. Ask the students of what vowel sound the igloo and person remind them. *I*. Repeat its short sound, *I—I—I—I*.

4. Hold up the decorated egg. Ask them of what vowel sound it reminds them. *E*. Repeat its short sound, *E—E—E—E*.

5. Hold up the artificial apple. Ask them of what short vowel sound the apple reminds them. *A*. Repeat it, *A—A—A—A*. Place the apple, egg, igloo, doughnut, and umbrella in the display area labeled "short vowel sounds."

6. One at a time, hold up a cardboard sign of each vowel letter. Ask the students to give each vowel letter's long sound.

7. One at a time, hold up a cardboard sign of each vowel letter. Ask the students to give each vowel letter's short sound.

8. Tell the students the display is no longer for just short vowel sounds but for both long and short vowel sounds. Put a new sign up that says, "long and short vowel sounds." Beside each object, place the vowel card: *A* beside apple, *E* beside egg, *I* beside igloo, *O* beside doughnut, and *U* beside umbrella. Use the display each day to quickly review the previously learned long and short vowel sounds.

9. Follow-up activity. Staple the vowel pictures made throughout Section 14 together.

Procedures Day Eight

1. Review the long and short vowel sounds, using the long and short vowel display.

2. Teach part of "The Vowel Song." Use the music scale below. Notice that no part of the mouth touches even though the mouth's shape will change.

3. Repeat what was done in number 2 above, but this time sing the short sound of the vowels using the music scale.

4. Sing the scale several times using long and short vowel sounds.

5. Follow-up activity. Have the students compile the vowel pictures they made into a booklet. Have them make a construction paper cover decorated with notes and the vowel letters. Staple the cover on their booklet.

Procedures Day Nine

1. Review the long and short vowel sounds using the vowel display.

2. Sing the long and short sounds using yesterday's music scale.

3. Teach "The Vowel Song" using the following words and music score.

The Vowel Song

Verse 1:

A, E, I, O, U
Hear our names.
Hear our names.
Vowels we are, oh yes.
A, E, I, O, U

Verse 2:

A, E, I, O, U
These are our long sounds.
Hear our long sounds.
Hear our long sounds.
A, E, I, O, U

Verse 3:

A, E, I, O, U
These are our short sounds.
Hear our short sounds.
Hear our short sounds.
A, E, I, O, U

Verse 4:

A, E, I, O, U
Apple, egg and igloo,
Ahhh and umbrella,
These help us remember,
A, E, I, O, U.

Verse 5:

A, E, I, O, U (long sounds)
A, E, I, O, U (short sounds)
Vowel sounds long and short,

Now we know them well.
We think you do, too.

The Vowel Song

Procedures for Day Ten

1. Review the long and short vowel sounds using the Vowel Display.

2. Practice "The Vowel Song."

3. Record the students singing "The Vowel Song." Listen to the recording.

4. Sing "The Vowel Song" to an audience.

Congratulations to you and your students! Your students know the information in the very important basic sections in Unit II. Go on to Unit III, Section 1. Allow additional time for the following instructor preparation.

UNIT III

USING THE CONSONANTS AND VOWELS TO DECODE WORDS AND THE NEXT MOST USED SIGHT WORDS

Background and Preparation for Teaching Unit III

In this unit you will teach sight words and phonetic decoding at the same time. This will give the students a reading vocabulary of about 65 percent of all words most used in written material.

The students are to continue finding patterns in words. These patterns are phonetic rules. It is important for your students to memorize sight words and to figure out words by using letter sounds and phonetic patterns (rules). They will also learn to add suffixes to words previously learned, forming new words.

In each lesson, you are given the information to evaluate and teach your students to find patterns, phonic rules, and use them to figure out new words. Teach carefully. Make sure the phonics skills and sight words are learned well.

If instructing a group: Make a chart to be used for the rest of the lessons. Put student names in two columns. This becomes the Buddy Partner Chart. It is posted, so everyone can see who their weekly partner is. It also assures them they will have an opportunity to work with other students during another week. Change this chart weekly by rotating one column on the chart. See the sample chart below.

Buddy Partner Chart—Sample for the First Eleven Weeks

A	B	
Katie	Joe	Make a name card
Robert	Daniel	for each student. Place them in
Ben	Trina	slots on a chart so they can be
Sara	Stevie	be moved. Move the column B
Mandy	Chris	cards down one slot each week.
		Column A remains the same.

Ethan	Jamie	For example, the first week Katie
Rachel B.	Jess	and Joe are buddy partners,
Kimberly	Nezzeray	and Robert and Daniel are
Jeffrey	Rachel H.	buddy partners. The second week
Sami	Saxon	Katie and Jasmine are buddy partners, and
Mikey	Jasmine	Robert and Joe are buddy partners.

When each person in column A has partnered with all the column B people, the cycle has been completed. Then put half of the column A name cards in column B, and half the column B name cards in column A so new buddy partnerships can be formed. The sample Buddy Partner Chart will then look like this.

Buddy Partner Chart—Sample for the Second Eleven Weeks

A	B	
Katie	Rachel B.	Continue rotating names in
Robert	Kimberly	column B by moving each name
Ben	Jeffrey	down one slot for the new week's
Sara	Sami	lesson. Each person in
Mandy	Mikey	column A will be a Buddy
Ethan	Jamie	Partner with everyone in
Joe	Jess	column A. Continue to change the
Daniel	Nezzeray	chart until all students have partnered
Trina	Rachel H.	with all the others.
Stevie	Saxon	
Chris	Jasmine	

If instructing a group or individual: Use the information in Section 2 to prepare for the first lesson. Follow the preparation steps outlined below. You will usually follow these same steps in preparation for each section.

1. Use four overhead transparencies and a permanent transparency marker to make most weeks' lessons.

2. On the first transparency, make a section called "Sight Word Practice." On it write sight words that need reviewing from previous lessons. See the sample below.

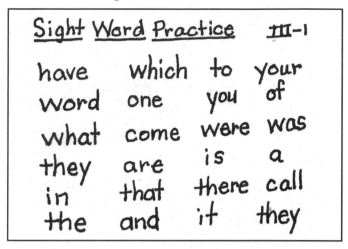

Sight Word Practice   III-1

have	which	to	your
word	one	you	of
what	come	were	was
they	are	is	a
in	that	there	call
the	and	it	they

3. On the second transparency make a section called Detective Decoding Practice. On it write the phonic words that need reviewing from previous lessons. See the sample below.

Detective Decoding   III-1
Practice

th   sh   wh   ch

ā   ē   ī   ō   ū

ă   ĕ   ĭ   ŏ   ŭ

from   they   yours

4. On the third transparency make a section called Detective Decoding Rule Search. On it, write the phonic words from Phonics Rule 1. Do not write the rule. Know the phonics rule well and be able to apply it so you can help the students figure out the rule. Then figure out the words using the phonics rule and recognize them instantly. See the sample below.

Detective Decoding Rule Search			III-1
that	hot	men	
them	his	but	
which	can	will	
when	has	sit	
let	get	got	
with	ten	not	
had	this	then	
him	stop	big	
did	than	run	

5. On the fourth transparency, write Detective Word Leaping. On it, write the challenge words that follow Phonics Rule 1.

Detective Word Leaping			III-1
wish	land	just	quit
six	left	well	cut
much	pick	spell	quick
went	back	fast	man
last	set	next	plant
list	hand	man	fish
miss	quack	quick	
tell	best	still	

6. Prepare a Parent/Student Reading Together Coupon. Copy to go home with the Buddy Partner Practice Sheet each week. See sample below.

Parent/Student Reading Together Coupon

Due back on Thursday, _____

_____ (student name) has gone over Unit ___, Section____assignment with me or another adult _____ times.

Comments:

Signed _____

On the back, write the book(s) name and pages read during the week.

7. Prepare a Buddy Partner Practice Sheet for the week's lessons. See the sample on the next page.

8. Each week make several copies of the Buddy Partner Practice Sheet and the Parent/Student Reading Together Coupon for the future.

9. Prepare a parent letter to go home on *only* the first Friday following Unit III, Section 2 lessons. See sample on pages 101. Write your own letter to make it more personal.

Buddy Partner Practice Sheet—Unit III, Section 2

Name_____

Sight Word Practice

Say these words as quickly as possible.

the	and	to	is	of	a
in	that	you	it	was	they
have	are	come	there	one	call
word	what	were	your	which	

Detective Decoding Practice

Say the long vowel sounds.
Say the short vowel sounds.

Aa, Ee, Ii, Oo, Uu

Detective Decoding Rule Search

Figure out these words by using Phonics Rule 1.

Phonics Rule 1: One vowel in a word with consonants on both sides of it, usually makes its short vowel sound.

that	with	his	this	but
not	when	had	can	stop
will	then	them	him	has
than	did	get	which	did
get	has	got	run	let
hot	ten	men	big	sit

Detective Word Leaping

Figure out more words by using Phonics Rule 1.

wish	list	pick	best	fast
cut	six	miss	back	just
man	help	much	tell	set
well	next	such	went	land
hand	spell	still	plant	last
left	quack	quick	quit	such

Sample Reading Packet Letter

(Date)

Dear Parents,

(student name) will be bringing a reading packet home each Friday, which will allow you to follow your child's reading progress and to assist him/her.

The packet will contain one or more of the following materials, which were used during the week:

1. Parent/Student Reading Together Coupon
2. New Sight Words (words to memorize)
3. Detective Decoding Word Search (words to read using a phonics rule)
4. Detective Word Leaping (more challenging words to read using a phonics rule)
5. A reading game
6. A book to read
7. Materials for the student to teach the parent

Your child will be pleased to share the newly learned information with you. He/she has been assigned to read the packet materials with an adult at least three times. Your child will be reinforced by your attention, interest, and positive comments. The importance you place on reading will be obvious. At the same time, you will be knowledgeable of your child's reading progress.

By the following week, day four, the students should return only the signed Parent/Student Reading Coupon together with any comments and observations you want to communicate to me. Keep the other papers in a notebook for reading reviews. By going through these periodically, you and your child will realize how much learning has occurred. Please help your child be responsible about returning the coupon every week.

Research indicates that reading ability develops more quickly when parents are involved. Please read to your child ten to twenty minutes a day. After learning to read, the child should also read to you. On the back of the coupon, please list the books your child read during the week.

I hope the material in the packet and the books you read together will provide some pleasurable, positive times for your family.

Please feel free to contact me with concerns or positive feedback. I will do the same with you. Communication between us can only enhance your child's reading progress.

Sincerely,
(teacher name)

Phonics Instruction: Rule 1

Instructor Background
Rule 1

If there is only one vowel in a short word with consonants on both sides of it, the vowel usually has its short sound as in the words s<u>a</u>ck and p<u>a</u>l.

Silly Story

Each vowel, A, E, I, O, or U, feels so comfortable when it's the only vowel in the word and there are consonants on both sides of it. When that happens, the vowel purrs its happy, comfortable short sound.

Detective Decoding Rule Search

that	with	his	this	but	not
when	had	can	stop	will	then
them	him	has	than	sit	big
which	did	get	men	got	run
let	hot	ten			

Detective Word Leaping

wish	list	pick	best	fast	cut
six	miss	back	just	man	help
much	tell	set	well	next	such
went	land	hand	spell	still	plant
last	left	quack	quick	quit	fish

This section will take one week to cover. Preparation time will be needed for making transparencies, Buddy Partner Practice Sheets, the Parent/Student Reading Together Coupon, and Parent Letter.

Procedures for Day One

1. With the students quickly review the overhead transparencies, Sight Word Practice and Detective Decoding Practice.

2. Display the overhead transparency Detective Decoding Rule Search. Tell the students they are the detectives, to put on their detective hats. They are to first search for what's alike about the words while they are repeating them after you.

3. Say a word; have the students repeat it.

4. Ask the students what they found alike about all the words. Help them discover the pattern. Using a temporary overhead marker, write the rule when the students discover it. Continue to use the temporary marker for any additional writing on the transparency. (The items written with temporary marker will later come off with clear water but leave what was written with permanent marker.)

5. Suggest the students check to see if this rule works with all the words. (Wording for the rule doesn't have to be the same if the meaning of the rule is correct. For instance, when there is a consonant, then a vowel, then a consonant, the vowel makes its short sound.) Go through each word, having students say it along with you. After each word, solicit student help, such as, "Is there only one vowel in the middle of the word?" "Yes." "Which vowel is it?" "*A*." "Then what sound should it have?" "Short *A* sound." "What sound does the short *A* vowel make?" "*A*." Mark the *A* using the short *A* symbol, saying, "This smile mark above the *A* tells us the vowel makes its short sound.

6. Say, "Let's say the words together and see if we were good detectives, if we found the rule." Be sure students don't sound each individual letter, but rather "smoosh" them together. (They like the word smoosh.) Move finger quickly under the word as students say it. If they have difficulty "smooshing" the letters together, have them use a hand to sweep through the air as you move your finger across the word, together repeating the words. (Have fun—be dramatic!) Try to develop this "smooshing" technique as early as possible with the students.

7. If the students didn't find the correct rule, repeat the procedure until the correct rule is found.

8. Tell the students the Silly Story about the rule.

Silly Story

Each vowel, A, E, I, O, or U, feels so comfortable when it's the only vowel in the word and there are consonants on both sides of it. When that happens, the vowel purrs its happy, comfortable short sound.

9. Have the students read the words without your help as you use the sweeping finger. After several lessons, ask one or more student volunteers to be the instructors for this step.

10. The words have been named four times now. Go over them one more time, pointing randomly.

Procedures for Day Two

1. Display the Detective Decoding Practice overhead transparency. Go over it quickly.

2. Display Detective Decoding Rule Search overhead transparency. Quickly review the new week's rule. Repeat the words several times in different ways.

3. These words should be easily read by the end of the week. Provide any extra practice *as needed*. Be creative. Use small group games or activities later in the day, too.

4. *If instructing a group:* Buddy partner the students using the Buddy Partner Chart on pages 95–96. Tell the students that each of them will buddy read with the assigned partner for the week, and that they will have a new buddy each week. The buddy is responsible to help his/her partner learn and to successfully read the Buddy Partner Practice Sheet. Have them try reading just one section at a time to the buddy, then the other buddy reads. Tell them that if a word is misread, say the word for the partner and help the buddy partner learn it. You will become a partner in case of absences.

   If instructing an individual: You and the student are always buddy partners, reading the Buddy Partner Practice Sheet together.

5. Explain the Buddy Partner Practice Sheet to the students. Give them each a Buddy Partner Practice Sheet for Section 2. With the assigned partner, have each student write his/her name at the top, then practice reading the Sight Word Practice, Detective Decoding Practice, and Detective Decoding Rule Search.

6. As the students buddy partner practice, oversee, assist, and note which items need reteaching. If a student needs considerable additional assistance, you may sit with the partners or work individually with the student.

7. When completed, have the students return the Practice Partner Sheet to you.

Procedures for Day Three

1. Display the Detective Decoding Rule Search overhead transparency. Go over the words with whatever deliberation is needed, depending upon the students and your observations on day two. Be creative, make it fun, make it reasonably quick to super quick. Plan to work individually with students having difficulty.

2. Display the Detective Word Leaping overhead transparency. Challenge the students to read the words to themselves first. Ask the students what decoding phonics rule each word followed. Then challenge the students to read the words with you as you sweep your finger across the words.

3. Go over the Detective Word Leaping list several times in several different ways, making it fun. By the end of the week these words should be either easily read or easily figured out.

4. Provide students with Buddy Partner practice time and the weekly Buddy Partner Practice Sheet. With the assigned partner, have each student practice everything on the sheet—the Sight Word Practice, Detective Decoding Practice, Detective Decoding Rule Search, and Detective Word Leaping.
   If instructing an individual: You are the student's partner.

5. Have the students return the Buddy Practice Partner Sheet to you.

Procedures for Day Four

1. Display Detective Decoding Rule Search overhead transparency. Go through it quickly.
2. Display Detective Word Leaping overhead transparency. Go through it several times.
3. Provide for buddy partner practice time using the same sheet as on the second and third days.
4. Have the students return the Buddy Practice Partner Sheet to you.
5. Provide fifteen to twenty minutes of independent reading time for the students, as well as reading games and activities.

Procedures for Day Five

Provide students with their Partner Practice Sheet with the Parent/Student Reading Together Coupon attached. (See page 99) Fill in the date due back, unit, and section numbers. Have each student write his/her name on the Parent/Student Reading Together Coupon.

If instructing an individual:

1. The student reads only to you while you evaluate. As you listen, make notes of the words, rules, and sounds with which the student needs additional help. Use these words, rules, and sounds for next week's review.
2. Give the student feedback on the way he/she worked with you during the week. Write a positive note on the Buddy Partner Practice Sheet.

If instructing a group:

Partners read the Buddy Partner Practice Sheet to each other making sure each is reading successfully. When buddy partners finish working with each other, they put their papers in a specific basket and begin independent silent reading, using the classroom library.

3. Get a set of buddy partners from the silent reading activity and their Buddy Partner Practice Sheets from the basket.
   a. One buddy partner has his/her buddy read from the Buddy Partner Practice Sheets for the instructor, helping the buddy as needed, then the other buddy partner has his/her buddy read from the Buddy Partner Practice Sheets for you.

b. As you listen to the Buddies read, note the words, rules, and sounds with which the student needs additional help. It is OK to interrupt the reading and send the buddy partners to work together more, especially if they weren't serious about their assignment to help each other learn. Listen to them again later. Recess time is an effective time since you were busy listening to others during class time.

c. Give the partners feedback on the way they worked together during the week. Write a positive note on the Partner Practice Sheet.

d. Have the partners return to silent reading while you continue to evaluate other students' progress.

e. If several students miss the same words, these words should be included on the next week's review lessons and activities. Also work at another time with a small group or an individual student if further repetition or review is needed.

If Instructing an Individual or a Group

1. Give the students the Parent/Student Reading Together Coupon with the Buddy Partner Practice Sheet attached. Explain it to the students. Tell the students they are to read the Buddy Partner Practice Sheet at home with their parents or another adult three times or more until they can say the words quickly. Their parents or other adult who reads with them fills in the Parent/Student Reading Together Coupon and signs it. The Buddy Partner Practice Sheet is to be kept in a folder or notebook at home to practice later. Tell them it is their responsibility to return the Parent/Student Reading Together Coupon by the following week's due date.

2. Tell the students you are sending the directions for their parents. Impress upon them how important it is that their parents see the letter. Give them each a letter. Read the letter to the students. See the sample letter on pages 101–102.

3. Help the students realize that each has a *responsibility* to return the Parent/Student Reading Together Coupon by the following week. Keep a record of the returned Parent/Student Homework Coupon and help the students develop a habit of doing this homework regularly. Go to Section 3 for the next week's lessons.

Phonics Instruction: Rule 2

Instructor Background
Rule 2

If there is only one vowel in a short word, and it's at the end of the word, the vowel usually has its long sound as in the words m<u>e</u> and cr<u>y</u>.

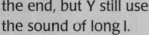

Silly Story

Whenever a vowel is all by itself in a very short word and is at the end of the word, it Is so proud it says its own name, which is its long sound.

Y at the end of a very short word has traded places with I who is too lonely at the end, but Y still uses the sound of long I.

The symbol to show that a vowel is saying its own name—called a long vowel sound—is a long straight line above the vowel.

Detective Decoding Rule Search

he	be	we	she	by	so
go	my	no	go	me	

Detective Word Leaping

why	try	fly	cry

This section will take one week to cover. Instructor preparation time will be needed for making transparencies, the Buddy Partner Practice Sheet, and the Parent/Student Reading Together Coupon. You will be following similar basic daily procedures as were outlined in Section 2.

Procedures for Day One

1. With the students, quickly review the words and phonics using the Sight Word Practice and Detective Decoding Practice overhead transparencies for this lesson.

2. Display the Detective Decoding Rule Search overhead transparency. Tell the students to put on their detective hats. They are to first search for what's alike about the words while they repeat them after you.

3. Say a word; the students repeat it.

4. Ask students what they found alike about all the words. Help the students discover the pattern. Using a temporary overhead marker, write the rule when the students discover it. You can continue to use the temporary marker for any additional writing on the transparency. (It will later come off with clear water in preparation for the next lesson, but leave what was written with permanent marker.)

5. Suggest the students check to see if this rule works with all the words. Wording for the rule doesn't have to be the same if it has the same meaning. Go through each word, having students say it along with you. After each word, solicit student help, such as, "How many vowels are in each word?" *One.* "Where is the vowel?" *At the end of the word.* "What sound does the vowel have?" *The long* A *sound.* Mark the *A* using the long symbol and

say, "This straight line above the vowel tells us the vowel makes its long sound."

6. Say, "Let's say the words together and see if we were good detectives, if we found the rule." Be sure the students don't sound each individual letter but rather "smoosh" them together. Move your finger under the word quickly as students say it. If they have difficulty "smooshing" the letters together, have them use a hand to sweep through the air as you move your finger across the word, together repeating the words. (Have fun—be dramatic!) Try to develop this "smooshing" technique as early as possible with the students.

7. If the students didn't find the correct rule, repeat the procedure until the correct rule is found.

8. Tell the students the Silly Story about the rule.

Silly Story

Whenever a vowel is all by itself in a very short word and is at the end of the word, it is so proud it says its own name, which is its long sound.

Y at the end of a very short word has traded places with I who is too lonely at the end, but Y still uses the sound of long I.

9. Have the students read the words without your help, as you use the sweeping finger. After several lessons, you may ask one or more student volunteers to be the instructors for this step.

10. The words have been named four times now. Go over them one more time, pointing randomly.

Procedures for Day Two

1. Display the Detective Decoding Practice overhead transparency. Go over it quickly.

2. Display Detective Decoding Rule Search overhead transparency. Quickly review the new week's rule. Repeat the words several times in different ways. These words should be easily read by the end of the week.

3. Provide extra practice *as needed*. Be creative. Use small group games or activities later in the day, too.

4. *If instructing a group:*

   Buddy partner the students using the Buddy Partner Chart. Remind them that each will buddy read with the assigned partner for the week and that a buddy is responsible to help his/her partner successfully read the Buddy Partner Practice Sheet. (You are a partner in case of absences. If a student needs considerable additional assistance, you may sit with partners or work individually with the student.) Remind them that one reads a section and then the other buddy reads the section. Tell them that if a word is misread, the other buddy should say the word for the partner and help the buddy partner learn it.

   If instructing an individual:

   You and the student are always buddy partners, reading the Buddy Partner Practice Sheet together.

5. Give each student a Buddy Partner Practice Sheet for section 3. Have each student write his/her name at the top, then with the assigned partner, practice reading the Sight Word Practice, Detective Decoding Practice, and Detective Decoding Rule Search.

7. As the students buddy partner practice reading to each other oversee, assist, and note items that need reteaching.

8. When completed, have the students return the Buddy Partner Practice Sheet to you.

Procedures for Day Three

1. Display the Detective Decoding Rule Search overhead transparency. Go over the words with whatever deliberation is needed, depending upon the students and your observations on day two. Be creative, make it fun—make it reasonably quick to super quick. Plan to work individually with students having difficulty.

2. Display the Detective Word Leaping overhead transparency. Challenge the students to read the words to themselves first. Ask the students what decoding phonics rule each word followed. Then challenge the students to read the words with you as you sweep your finger across the words.

3. Go over the Detective Word Leaping list several times in several different ways, making it fun. These words should be easily read or easily figured out by the end of the week.

4. Provide students with Buddy Partner practice time and the weekly Buddy Partner Practice Sheet. With the assigned partner, have each student practice everything on the sheet—the Sight Word Practice, Detective Decoding Practice, Detective Decoding Rule Search, and Detective Word Leaping.

5. Have the students return the Buddy Practice Partner Sheet to you.

Procedures for Day Four

1. Display the Detective Decoding Rule Search overhead transparency. Go through it quickly.

2. Display the Detective Word Leaping overhead transparency. Go through it several times.

3. Provide for buddy partner practice time using the same sheet as on days three and four.

4. Have the students return the Buddy Partner Practice Sheet.

5. Provide fifteen to twenty minutes of independent reading time for the students, as well as reading games and activities. Use games played previously or see Games in the Index for additional ideas.

Procedures for Day Five

If instructing an individual:

1. Provide the student with a Buddy Partner Practice Sheet with the Parent/Student Reading Together Coupon attached. Fill in the date due back and the unit and section numbers. Have the students write their name on the Parent/Student Reading Together Coupon.

2. The student reads to you while you evaluate. As you listen, note the words, rules, and sounds with which the student needs additional help. Use these words, rules, and sounds for next week's review.

3. Give the student feedback on the way he/she worked with you during the week Write a positive note on the Buddy Partner Practice Sheet.

If instructing a group:

1. Provide students with a Buddy Partner Practice Sheet with the Parent/Student Reading Together Coupon attached. Fill in the date due back and the unit and section numbers. Have the students write their name on the Parent/Child Reading Together Coupon.

2. Partners read the Buddy Partner Practice Sheet to each other making sure each is reading successfully.

3. When buddy partners finish working with each other they put their papers in a specific basket and begin independent silent reading, using the classroom library.

4. Get a set of buddy partners from the silent reading activity and their Buddy Partner Practice Sheets from the basket.

    a. One buddy partner has his/her buddy read from the Buddy Partner Practice Sheets for the instructor, helping the buddy as needed. The other buddy partner has his/her buddy read from the Buddy Partner Practice Sheets for you.

    b. As you listen to the buddies read, note the words, rules, and sounds with which the student needs additional help. (It is OK to interrupt the reading and send the buddy partners to work together more, especially if they weren't serious about their assignment to help each other learn. Listen to them again later. Recess time is an effective time since you were busy listening to others during class time.)

    c. Give the partners feedback on the way they worked together during the week.

    Write a positive note on the Partner Practice Sheet.

5. Have the partners return to silent reading while you continue to evaluate other students' progress.

6. If several students miss the same words, these words should be included on the next week's review lessons and activities. Work with a small group or an individual student at another time if further repetition or review is needed.

If instructing an individual or a group:

Give the students the Parent/Student Reading Together Coupon with the Buddy Partner Practice Sheets attached. Remind the students they are to read the Buddy Partner Practice Sheet at home with parents or another adult three times or more until they can quickly say the words. Then their parents or the other adult that read with them, fills in the Parent/Student Reading Together Coupon and signs it. The Buddy Partner Practice Sheet is to be kept in a folder or notebook at home to practice later. Remind them it is their responsibility to return the Parent/Student Reading Together Coupon by the following week's due date. Go to Section 4 for the next week's lessons.

Phonics Instruction: Rule 3

Instructor Background
Rule 3

In a short word, if there is only one consonant between a single vowel and an *E* at the end of a word, the single vowel usually has its long sound and the *E* at the end is silent as in the words m<u>u</u>l<u>e</u> and s<u>a</u>l<u>e</u>.

To mark the silent *E* and long vowel sound, draw a vertical line through the *E* and hop the line over the consonant to make the symbol for a long vowel sound, a straight line over the vowel.

Silly Story

E loves to practice its jumping skills. E needs a running start, so it can only practice its jumping skills when it is at the end of a word. E has a lot of trouble jumping over two consonants, so when there's only one consonant to jump over, E takes a running jump. There it goes, right over the consonant. E lands right on the only other vowel in the word and makes the vowel say its name. (That's the vowel's long sound.) Then E goes back to the end of the word. It loves it there, because it can rest silently.

By the way, no matter how hard E practices, it hardly ever manages to jump over two consonants in front of it. It doesn't make any difference though, if there are one, two, or three consonants in front of the other vowel in the word.

Detective Decoding Rule Search

use	these	more	time	write	make
like	made	name	five	came	take

Detective Word Leaping

line	same	here	home	page	gave
place	while	close	life	those	side
mile	white	state	late	face	nice
rose					

Procedures

This section will take one week to cover. There will be instructor preparation time needed for making the transparencies, the Buddy Partner Practice Sheet, and the Parent/Student Reading Together Coupon, pages 99 to 100.

Follow the same daily procedures as were outlined in Unit III, Section 2. Go to Section 5 for the next week's lessons, pages 104 to 108.

Phonics Instruction: Rule 4

Instructor Background
Rule 4

If the only vowel in a very short word is at the beginning of the word, that vowel usually has its short sound as in the words ash and itch.

Silly Story

Whoopee! The vowel letter notices it is the only vowel in the word and it got to be the first letter in the word. Thank goodness, E is not at the end wanting to hop over the consonant and change it to its long sound! The consonant is feeling so comfortable and happy that it purrs its short sound.

The vowel doesn't care how many consonants are behind it.

Detective Decoding Practice

as	at	on	an	if	up
and	in	is	it	its	

Detective Word Leaping

end	ask	off	us	add

Procedures

This section will take one week to cover. There will be instructor preparation time needed for making transparencies, the Buddy Partner Practice Sheets, and the Parent/Student Reading Together Coupon, pages 99 to 100. Follow the same daily procedures as were outlined in Unit III, Section 2, pages 104 to 108. Go to Section 6 for the next week's lessons.

Phonics Instruction: Rules 5 And 6

Instructor Background
Rule 5

The two vowels *AY* or *AI* together in a word usually have the long *A* sound, while the *Y* or *I* is silent as in st<u>ay</u> and r<u>ai</u>n.

Silly Story

Remember how A and Y are sometimes together at the end of a word. And how Y told A it could say its long sound? Well, sometimes AY got put into the middle of a word. Y wanted out of there! It was too crowded for Y!

Remember how I said it didn't want to be at the end of a word because it was lonely? Well, I told Y whenever it was crowded into the middle of a word, it would be happy to take its place. And I still let A say its long sound.

Detective Decoding Word Search
    way   day   may   rain

Detective Word Leaping
    say   play   away

Rule 6

The two vowels *OW* often have the sound of *OW!* as in h<u>ow</u> and d<u>ow</u>n. Sometimes *OU* also has the sound of *OW!* as in h<u>ou</u>se. (Rule 27, page 161, has more about the *OU* sounds.)

Silly Story

O and W both take so much room when they are together, that they often bump into each other. You can hear them make the sound, "Ow!"

Detective Decoding Word Search
    how   down   now

Procedures

This section will take one week to cover. There will be instructor preparation time needed for making transparencies, the Buddy Partner Practice Sheets, and the Parent/Student Reading Together Coupon, pages 97 to 100.

Follow the same daily procedures as were outlined in Unit III, Section 2, pages 104 to 108, except use the words from both vowel rule lists, mixing the words up. Tell the students they are getting to be so good, they just might find two different rules. Go to Section 7 for the next week's lessons.

Phonics Instruction: Rules 7 and 8

Instructor Background
Rule 7

The two letters *OR* together often have the sound of the word or as in f<u>or</u> and st<u>or</u>y.

Silly Story

The letter R is usually bossy to the vowel in front of it. For instance, R makes the O change its sound, so Rs sound is heard better. Then Rs nickname is Bossy R.

Detective Decoding Rule Search
   for   or

Detective Word Leaping
   form   story

Rule 8

The two letters *IR, ER,* and *UR* usually have the sound as in the words h<u>er</u>, sh<u>ir</u>t, and f<u>ur</u>.

Silly Story

Remember about the letter R usually being Bossy R to the vowel in front of it. Well, when E, I, or U are in front of

---

> Bossy R, it makes them change their sound so Rs sound is heard better so ER, IR, and UR sound a little bit like a dog's growl. Oh, that Bossy R!

Detective Decoding Rule Search
   her   first

Detective Word Leaping
    turn   girl   hurt

Procedures

This section will take one week to cover. There will be instructor preparation time needed for making transparencies, the Buddy Partner Practice Sheets, and the Parent/Student Reading Together Coupon, pages 97 to 100.

Follow the same procedures for each day as were outlined in Unit III, Section 2, pages 104 to 108, except use the words from both lists, mixing the words up. Tell them to find the rules for this week's words. Go to Section 8 for the next week's lessons.

Phonics Instruction: Rule 9 and Sections 2 Through 8 Review

Instructor Background
Rule 9

When the letters *AL* are together, the *A* usually has the sound as in al̲l̲. Sometimes the *L* makes its sound as in sma̲l̲l̲ and ha̲l̲t. Sometimes the *L* is silent when followed by a *K* as in wa̲l̲k̲ and ta̲l̲k̲.

Silly Story

When A and L walk together with A going first, A gets shy and says, "Ah…." Sometimes L makes its regular sound, but sometimes L is speechless. Sometimes K tags along behind A and L. K likes to make its sound, so L is happy to have K there, especially when L is speechless.

Detective Decoding Rule Search

   all   call   fall

Detective Word Leaping

   also   small   always   walk   talk

Procedures

There will be additional instructor preparation time needed for making transparencies, the Buddy Partner Practice Sheets, and the Parent/Student Reading Together Coupon.

Teaching this vowel rule will *not* take one week to cover. In addition to the usual transparencies for the lesson, make a transparency copy of Appendixes D and E. The students are to practice recalling each word as quickly as possible, sounding out (decoding) words only if necessary.

For the Buddy Partner Practice Sheet, include vowel Rule 9 words from Detective Decoding Rule Search and Detective Word Leaping. Also copy Appendixes D and E. The owner of this book has permission to make copies for the use by the students.

Be sure the students realize how many words they now know. Tell the students their parents will also be very proud of how well they can do.

Congratulations! Now *all* of the words most used in writing have been memorized. The phonics rules that can be used to figure out (decode) many words have been learned. In addition, many words in the next group of most used words are now learned.

Your students can now comfortably read easy materials. Continue to encourage your students to do lots of reading with you, others, and alone. Play the Puff Game, then go to Section 9 for the next week's lessons.

Puff Game

Object of Game: To provide a fun way for students to have additional memorization practice on the basic sight words

Players: Three to six is the ideal number, but more can play if more cards are added.

Supplies:

- At least thirty-six word cards that were previously used for learning the sight words during the "Memory" game. You may have duplicate words. Each card should have one word printed on it.

- Four cards of the same size and color with the word "Puff" written on each card and two cards of the same size and color with the word "Save" written on them

- A simple oven timer

- A plastic or cloth bag

Setup: Students sit in a circle. Place all the word cards, along with the "Puff" and "Save" cards, in the bag. Mix them up well. Set the timer for three to six minutes.

The Play: The first player pulls a card from the bag and reads it aloud. Other players determine whether the word was said correctly. If a player reads a card correctly, that player may choose to stop his turn or to continue drawing cards and reading them for as long as desired. When the player chooses to stop his turn, it is the next player's turn.

If a word is read incorrectly, the player keeps the cards he has already won, but his turn is over. The card that was read incorrectly goes back into the bag. Mix the cards. The next player takes a turn.

If a player draws a "Puff" card, all of that player's word cards and the "Puff" card are tossed back into the bag. The cards are mixed within the bag. The next player takes a turn.

If a player draws a "Save" card, he saves it for future use, but his turn is over. The next player takes a turn.

In a future turn, if a player who draws a "Puff" card already has a "Save" card, he tosses only the "Save" and "Puff" cards back into the bag, keeping the cards he has read correctly. His turn is over.

Ending the Game: Play ends instantly when the timer buzzes. Each player counts the cards in his possession. Each card counts as 1 point. If a player still has a "Save" card, it counts 2 points. The top scorer wins.

Variations:

1. Vary the number of word cards, "Puff" cards, "Save" cards, or the length of the game.

2. Play a longer, more competitive cumulative game. Load the bag with a large number of cards. Determine how long the whole game will be (e.g., ten or twenty minutes). Set the timer for four to seven minutes for the first round. When the buzzer goes off, players keep the cards they have won in their own separate piles. All the "Save" cards go back into the bag. Play the second game. When the buzzer goes off, each player adds the cards he has won to his permanent pile but throws all "Save" cards back into the bag. Continue playing until time is up for the whole game. Each card in the permanent piles is worth 1 point. Each "Save" card is worth 2 points.

Suffix Instruction: Rules 10 Through 18

Instructor Background

This section will take one week to cover. There will be instructor preparation time needed for making transparencies, the Buddy Partner Practice Sheets, and the Parent/Student Reading Together Coupon.

By adding the common suffixes of *S, ES, ED,* and *ING* to some of the words included in Unit II, Sections 4 through 14, and Unit III, Sections 2 through 8, the students will learn how to use suffixes, review sight words, and learn new words.

When adding a suffix, the original word is called a *base or root word*. Use both terms so the student is familiar with both.

Charts A and B include the base words with the suffixes and are for the instructor's reference. Charts A-1 and B-1, which have only the base words, are for the instructors to copy onto a transparency.

Suffix Rules Used With Charts A, A-1, B, and B-1

A suffix is an ending added onto a base word.

Rule 10

Most of the time, just add the suffix if a short base word ends with two consonants, two vowels or two vowels before a single consonant as in walk<u>ed</u>, show<u>s</u> and load<u>ing</u>.

Rule 11

Suffix *S* has the *sound* of the letter *S* as in number<u>s</u> and play<u>s</u>. It is not a syllable. (See page 187 for syllable definition.)

Rule 12

The suffix *ES* may be added to a base word that ends with the voiceless sound of *O, S, SH, CH,* or *J* as in bush<u>es</u> and wish<u>es</u>. The *ES* sounds like the letter *S'* <u>name</u> except when it follows *O*. Then *ES* often has the <u>sound</u> of the letter *S*. Suffix *ES* is usually a syllable.

Rule 13

Suffix *ED* is added to a base word that ends with a vowel or voiced consonant sound. The suffix *ED* then has the *D* sound as in play<u>ed</u>, fill<u>ed</u>, and lean<u>ed</u>. This is the way the suffix *ED* is used most of the time. It is not a syllable.

Rule 14

Suffix *ED* is added to a base word that ends with a voiceless consonant sound. The suffix *ED* then has the *T* sound as in help<u>ed</u>, look<u>ed</u>, and wish<u>ed</u>. This is the way the suffix *ED* is used some of the time. It is not a syllable.

Rule 15

Suffix *ED* is added to a base word that ends with the *D* or *T* sound. The suffix *ED* then sounds like the boy's name, Ed, as in want<u>ed</u>, shout<u>ed</u>, and load<u>ed</u>. This is the way the suffix *ED* is used the least. It is a syllable.

Rule 16

Suffix *ING* has the sound as in start<u>ing</u> and bark<u>ing</u>. Suffix *ING* is a syllable.

Rule 17

Silent *E* is removed, dropped, from the end of a base word if a suffix with a vowel at the beginning is added as in lin<u>ed</u> and fil<u>ing</u>. Now there is only one consonant between the vowel in the middle of the base word and the vowel at the beginning of a suffix. This usually indicates there *had been* a silent *E* at the end of the base word, and the vowel in the middle will have its long sound.

Rule 18

Silent E sometimes has two jobs at the end of a base word. It may indicate the vowel in the middle has a long vowel sound and that *C* or *G* has a soft sound as in pag<u>ed</u> and fac<u>es</u>.

Procedures for Day One

1. With a sheet of paper, cover the Suffix Magic Chart A-1 transparency from the headings on down. Display the overhead transparency.

2. Explain that a suffix is a part added to the end of a word. That word is called a base word because it doesn't have anything added at its ending or beginning.

3. Tell the students they will not be detectives today but magicians and to please put on their magician's hats and be ready to change a base word they already know into new words.

4. Move the sheet of paper below the first word. Ask the students to use their magic with suffix *S* and the base word to make a new word. When the new word is said, ask to have it spelled. Write the word under the suffix *S* column. Continue down the column. The last word, go, uses the suffix *ES*. Not all the words will use all the suffixes. Help them discover this.

5. For the base word go, tell the following Silly Story.

Silly Story

One morning E saw O, S, SH, CH, and J chatting together about how much S, SH, CH, and J sounded alike. When they invited E to join them, E tried sounding each of their sounds. "What a grand discovery you have made!" he said with pride. "Yes," they agreed, "it is wonderful, but it also gives us all the same problem. You see, when S is a suffix and wants to come after us when we are in a base word, we all sound awful. Just try it, E." E tried the suffix S on the end of bus—buss, wishs, bunchs and bridges. E noticed the words sounded better when E stayed in bridge before the suffix S was added. E tried itself in the word buses, wishes and bunches. Wow! The faces of S, SH, CH, and J beamed with happiness. From then on, when E heard the sound of S, SH, CH, and J at the end of a base words he joined with S to make the suffix ES.

"Do it for me, too, E," pleaded O. Now, O seldom is at the end of a word, but when it is, Suffix S changes its sound, like in the words go and no. Suffix S changed O to a short sound, gos and nos. E certainly would help, but with only the <u>sound</u> of S. From then on, when E saw O at the end of a base word E joined with S to make the suffix ES, but with the <u>sound</u> of S.

6. Continue across the transparency in the same manner. Follow the same procedure with suffix *ED* and suffix *ING* columns.

7. Have the "magicians" read across the completed rows along with you. First read the base word and then the newly created "magic" words. Have fun along with them.

8. Help them realize they didn't have to change many base words. See if they can figure out why.

Suffix Magic Chart A

Base Words	Suffix s or es	Suffix ed	Suffix ing
number	numbers	numbered	numbering
find	finds		finding
out			outing
water	waters	watered	watering
look	looks	looked	looking
be			being
word	words	worded	wording
see	sees		seeing
call	calls	called	calling
fall	falls		falling
part	parts	parted	parting
long	longs	longed	longing
end	ends	ended	ending
pick	picks	picked	picking
list	lists	listed	listing
go	goes		going

Suffix Magic Chart A-1

Base Words	Suffix s or es	Suffix ed	Suffix ing
number			
find			
out			
water			
look			
be			
word			
see			
call			
fall			
part			
long			
end			
pick			
list			
go			

Procedures for Day Two

1. With a sheet of paper, cover the Transparency Suffix Magic Chart B-1 from the headings on down. Display the overhead transparency.

2. Ask the students to explain about base words and suffixes. If necessary, help them by giving them clues and additional information.

3. Display the entire overhead transparency. Ask the students what pattern is in the words. Tell them you wonder if there will still be a pattern after they add the suffixes.

4. Tell the students they will be magicians again, to please put on a magician's hat and be ready to use the strongest magic on the base words.

5. Put the sheet of paper below the first word. Ask the students to use magic with S or *ES* and the base word to make a new word. When the new word is said, ask them how to spell it. Write the word under the suffix *S/ES* column. Most likely they will not spell it correctly. Tell them, "I forgot something! The wizard told me a new Silly Story to tell his magicians."

Silly Story

When E is at the end of a word, it likes being the only vowel there. E doesn't want another vowel to join it at the end of a word, because then E couldn't rest silently. E would have to change its sound.

When suffix ES or ED comes to join E at the end of a word, that puts another vowel, E, next to E. E just wants to rest silently, not to change its sound, so E usually just drops and goes away.

When suffix ING comes to the end of a word to join E, that puts the vowel I next to E. Poor E, it just wants to rest silently, but again E usually just drops and goes away.

6. Tell the second Silly Story about silent *E*.

7. Ask the students to try their magic again and tell them this is harder magic. As they spell each word, write it in the correct column. Do the same with suffix *ED* and suffix *ING*. Not all words will use all the suffixes.

8. Continue on down the transparency in the same manner.

9. Ask them what pattern(s) they discovered.

10. Have the "magicians" read across the rows along with you. First read the base word and then the newly created "magic" words. Have fun along with them.

Suffix Magic Chart B

Base Words	Suffix s or es	Suffix ed	Suffix ing
line	lines	lined	lining
time	times	timed	timing
write	writes		writing
make	makes		making
like	likes	liked	liking
come	comes		coming
take	takes		taking
face	faces	faced	facing
place	places	placed	placing

Suffix Magic Chart B-1

Base Words	Suffix s or es	Suffix ed	Suffix ing
line			
time			
write			
make			
like			
come			
take			
face			
place			

Procedures for Day Three

1. Along with the students review overhead transparencies A-1 and B-1 by reading across the rows.

2. Have the students buddy partner practice using a Buddy Partner Practice Sheet copied from Suffix Magic Charts A and B.

Procedures for Day Four

1. Introduce the students to the Magic Suffix Brew game. Tell the students the wizard dumped all the new base words with suffixes, which they magically created, into the pot to make magic brew. The wizard wants the words to simmer in the brew so he can use the brew when he returns.

2. Have them begin to play the game with you.

3. Once the game is learned, have the students play in groups of three to six. You play if a single student is being tutored.

Preparation: Write the words with suffixes from Magic Suffix Chart A and Magic Suffix Chart B on individual small cards. Make several sets. Students can help write the words. All cards are tossed into a magic brew pot. Cards saying "puff" are also placed in the "pot" along with other cards that say "save."

Game object: The object of the game is for the group to weaken the magic brew's strength by removing most of its words before the wizard returns. Set a timer to ring in twenty to thirty minutes to indicate when the wizard is returning. (You may manipulate the game's length by putting in fewer word cards or by changing the length of time.)

Procedures: The first player takes a card from the magic brew pot and reads it aloud. The other game players determine if the word is read correctly. If read correctly, that player may choose to stop his/her turn or to continue playing as long as desired, naming each word pulled from the magic brew pot. If a word is read incorrectly the player keeps the cards named, but his/her turn is over. If a "puff" card is drawn, all that player's words and the "puff" card are tossed back into the magic brew pot. That player's turn is over. If a "saved" card is drawn, the player keeps the cards already correctly named and the "saved" card. That player's turn is over. In a future turn, if a "puff" card is drawn by a player who has a "saved" card, he/she may save the cards by throwing both the "puff" and "saved" cards into the magic brew pot. The player keeps all the cards he/she has read correctly. That player's turn is over.

Conclusion: When the timer rings, the game is over. If the players have removed most of the cards, the wizard can't use the brew.

Celebrate! If most of the cards are gone from the pot, the wizard can't use the weakened brew.

4. Provide time for silent reading.

Procedures for Day Five

1. The students write their name on the Parent/Student Reading Together Coupon then buddy partner practice together.

2. When finished, the students go to silent reading.

3. Buddy partners read the sheet to you when asked. Record the more difficult words and save them for later review.

4. The students take the Parent/Student Reading Together Coupon packet home to go over with parents and return the following week. Go to Unit IV, Section 1 for the next week's lessons.

UNIT IV

MORE OF THE MOST USED PHONICS RULES AND THE NEXT MOST USED SIGHT WORDS

Sight Word and Phonics Instruction: Rules 19 and 20

Instructor Background
Rule 19

The consonant *C* immediately followed by an *E, I, or Y* usually has a soft *S* sound as in <u>ce</u>nter and <u>cy</u>cle.

Rule 20

The consonant *C* <u>not</u> immediately followed by an *E, I,* or *Y* usually has the sound of *K* as in <u>ca</u>t and cy<u>cle</u>.

Silly Story

The letter C had no sound of its own, poor C. C was so sad and tried so hard to make a sound of its own. (1) Then C remembered a story Momma Cat had read. It was about a cat who copied the sounds of other animals. Here is the story. "First Copy Cat copied the sound of a rooster, then a pig, a horse, and a mule. Next he walked into the forest and copied the sound of a bird and a squirrel."

Letter C thought, Mmmmm...maybe I could be a Copy Cat and copy other letter sounds. (2) I'll ask my best friends, S and K if I can copy their sounds." (3) Sure enough! Both S and K wanted to share their sounds. S said that whenever C had an E, I, or Y following it, C could copy its soft sound... ssss (as in the word soft.) (4) K thought that was a good idea, so he said C could also copy its sound if an E, I, or Y didn't follow C. C gave S and K a big smile, a big thank you, and a big hug. C was a happy Copy Cat. K and S were happy they could help C.

New Sight Words

great	new	put	where
does	picture	only	through

Detective Decoding Rule Search

came	because	picture	can
call	come	could	place
sentence	cut	lose	face

Detective Word Leaping

cold	second	music	color
country	school	car	carry
once	city	clean	

Procedures

This section will take one week to cover. There will be instructor preparation time needed for making transparencies, the Buddy Partner Practice Sheet, and the Parent/Student Reading Together Coupon. We will now add a New Sight Words transparency and instruction. For your convenience, the full daily procedures are outlined below.

Procedures for Day One

1. With the students quickly review the more difficult words previously taught, using the Sight Word Practice overhead transparency made for this lesson.

2. Display the transparency New Sight Words.

3. *If instructing a group:*

Move through the lesson steps quickly to keep everyone's attention. Repeat each word a minimum of five times during each initial lesson in order to give the students a chance to memorize. Before information is learned well, it must be repeated at least five times within a relatively short time. Information will be remembered even better if it is repeated using the way the students learn best.

   a. Using a finger, pointer, or hand, sweep from left to right under the first word as you say it. Students say the word. Say the next word, have the students repeat; say the next word, have the students repeat. Continue through all the words on the list. If you hear a word misspoken, simply repeat the word, then have the students repeat.

   b. Repeat the directions above but more quickly.

   c. Point to the words randomly; you and the students say each word.

   d. Point to the words randomly and ask those wearing red (or any classification) to say the words.

   e. Have brown-eyed students say the word with teacher; blue-, hazel-, green-, and gray-eyed students repeat.

If instructing an individual:

Move through the lesson steps quickly to keep the student's attention. Always repeat each word a minimum of five times during each initial lesson in order to give the student a chance to memorize. Before information is *well* learned, it must be repeated at least five times within a relatively short time. Information will be remembered even better if it is repeated using the way the student learns best.

   a. Using a finger, pointer, or hand, sweep from left to right under the first word as you say it. Have the student say the word. Say the next word, have the student repeat. Say the next word, then have the student repeat. Continue through all the words on the list. If you hear a word misspoken, repeat it, then have the student repeat it.

   b. Repeat the directions above, but more quickly.

    c. Have the student point to words he/she knows and say them. You repeat.

    d. You point to words the student omitted and say them. The student repeats.

    e. Point to the words randomly, both you and the student say the word.

4. Display the overhead transparency Detective Decoding Rule Search. Tell the students to put on their detective hats. They are to search for the pattern in the words and the vowel rule.

    a. Say a word, then have the students repeat it.

    b. Ask the students what they found alike about all the words. Help them discover the pattern. Using a temporary overhead marker, write the rule when the students discover it. Continue to use the temporary marker for any additional writing on the overhead transparency. (It will later come off with clear water in preparation for the next lesson, leaving what was written with permanent marker.)

    c. Suggest they check to see if this rule works with all the words. Wording for the rule isn't important as long as the meaning is correct. Go through each word, having the students say it along with you. After each word solicit student help, such as, "What vowel followed the letter *C*?" "What sound did the *C* make, S or *K*?" Write *S* or *K* above the *C*.

    d. Say, "Let's say the words together and see if we were good detectives, if we found the rule." Do the words where *C* made the sound of *S*, then do the words where *C* made the sound of *K*. Write each word in an *S* or a *K* column as they are read.

    e. If the students didn't find the correct rule, repeat the procedure until the correct rule is found.

    f. Ask the students to repeat the Silly Story about the rule.

5. Have the students read the words without your help, as you use a sweeping finger. After several lessons, you may ask one or more student volunteers to be the instructors for this step.

6. The words have been named four times now. Go over them one more time, pointing randomly.

Procedures for Day Two

1. Display the Sight Word Practice and New Sight Words transparencies one at a time. Go over them with as much speed or deliberation as the students need.

2. If there are decoding words that need practice, display the Detective Decoding Practice overhead transparency. Go over it with as much speed or deliberation as the students need.

3. Display the Detective Decoding Rule Search overhead transparency. Quickly review the new week's rule. Repeat the words several times in different ways.

4. Provide any extra practice *as needed*. Be creative. Use small group games or activities later in the day, too.

5. *If instructing a group:*

   Buddy partner the students using the Buddy Partner Chart. Remind the students that each of them will buddy read with the assigned partner for the week and that they will have a new buddy each week. The buddy is responsible to help his/her partner learn and to successfully read the Buddy Partner Practice Sheet. Remind them to read just one section at a time to the buddy, then the other buddy reads. Remind them that if a word is misread, say the word for the partner and help the buddy partner learn it.

   If instructing an individual:

   You and the student are buddy partners, reading the Buddy Partner Practice Sheet together.

6. Give each student a Buddy Partner Practice Sheet for Unit IV, Section 1. With the assigned partner, have each student write his/her name at the top, then practice reading the Sight Word Practice, New Sight Words, Detective Decoding Practice, and Detective Decoding Rule Search.

7. As the students buddy partner practice reading to each other, oversee, assist, and note items that need reteaching. If a student needs considerable additional assistance, you may sit with the partners or work individually with the student.

8. When completed, have the students return the Buddy Partner Practice Sheet to you.

Procedures for Day Three

1. Display the New Sight Words and Detective Decoding Rule Search overhead transparencies. Go over the words with whatever deliberation is needed, depending upon the students and your observations from Day Two. Be creative, make it fun, and make it reasonably to super quick. Plan to work individually with students having difficulty.

2. Display Detective Word Leaping overhead transparency. Challenge the students to read the words to themselves first. Ask the students what decoding phonics rule each word followed. Then challenge the students to read the words with you as you sweep your finger across the words.

3. Go over the Detective Word Leaping list several times in several different ways, making it fun. Provide students with buddy partner practice time and his/her weekly Buddy Partner Practice Sheet. With the assigned partner, have each student practice everything on the sheet—the Sight Word Practice, Detective Decoding Practice, New Sight Words, Detective Decoding Rule Search, and Detective Word Leaping.

4. Have the students return the Buddy Practice Partner Sheet to you.

Procedures for Day Four

1. Display the New Sight Words and Detective Decoding Rule Search overhead transparencies. Go through them quickly.

2. Display the Detective Word Leaping overhead transparency. Go through it several times.

3. Provide for buddy partner practice time using the same Buddy Partner Practice Sheet as on the second and third days.

4. Have the students return the Buddy Partner Practice Sheet to you.

5. Provide fifteen to twenty minutes of independent reading time for the students as well as reading games and activities.

Procedures for Day Five

If instructing an individual:

1. Provide student with a Buddy Partner Practice Sheet, with the Parent/Student Reading Together Coupon attached. Fill in the date due back and the unit and section numbers. Have the student write his/her name on the Parent/Child Reading Together Coupon.

2. The student reads to you while you evaluate. As you listen, note the words, rules, and sounds with which the student needs additional help. Use these words, rules, and sounds for the following week's review.

3. Give the student feedback on the way he/she worked with you during the week. Write a positive note on the Buddy Partner Practice Sheet.

If instructing a group:

1. Provide students with the Buddy Partner Practice Sheet, with the Parent/Student Reading Together Coupon attached. Fill in the date due back and the unit and section numbers. Have the students write their name on the Parent/Student Reading Together Coupon.

2. Partners read the Buddy Partner Practice Sheet to each other making sure each is reading successfully.

3. When buddy partners finish working with each other they put their papers in a specific basket and begin independent silent reading, using the classroom library.

4. Get a set of buddy partners from silent reading and their Buddy Partner Practice Sheets from the basket.

5. One buddy partner has his/her buddy read from the Buddy Partner Practice Sheets for you, helping the buddy as needed, then the other buddy partner has his/her buddy read from the Buddy Partner Practice Sheets for you.

6. As you listen to the buddies read, note the words, rules, and sounds with which the student needs additional help. (It is OK to interrupt the reading and send the buddy partners to work together more, especially if they weren't serious about their assignment to help each other learn. Listen to them again later, such as at recess time.)

7. Give the students feedback on the way the partners worked together during the week. Write a positive note on the Partner Practice Sheet.

8. Have the partners return to silent reading while you continue to evaluate other students' progress.

9. If several students miss the same words, these words should be included on the next week's review lessons and activities. Work at another time with a small group or an individual student if further repetition or review is needed.

If Instructing an Individual or a Group

Give the students the Parent/Student Reading Together Coupon with the Buddy Partner Practice Sheets attached. Remind the students they are to read the Buddy Partner Practice Sheet at home with parents or another adult three times or more until they can quickly say the words. Then their parents or the other adult who reads with them can fill in the Parent/Student Reading Together Coupon and sign it. The Buddy Partner Practice Sheet is to be kept in a folder or notebook at home to practice later. Remind them it is their responsibility to return the Parent/Student Reading Together Coupon by the due date. Go to Section 2.

Sight Word and Phonics Instruction: Rules 21 and 22

Instructor Background
Rule 21

The consonant *G* immediately followed by an *E, I,* or *Y* often has the soft sound of *J* as in <u>gi</u>raffe and <u>gy</u>psy.

Rule 22

The consonant *G* <u>not</u> immediately followed by an *E, I,* or *Y* often has its own hard sound as in <u>ga</u>te and <u>gr</u>ass.

Silly Story

The letter G liked the plan that S and K had to help C. G had always admired the sound of J, so G asked J if he could copy the same idea. G explained the plan. If G had an E, I or Y following it, J would let G make its J sound. J agreed to the plan but only if G would make its own hard sound when other letters were following it. G happily agreed. But I'll tell you a secret! The plan doesn't always work for G. I wonder why?

New Sight Words

another	again	little	work
before	know	right	even

Detective Decoding Rule Search

good	great	get	page
girl	gave		

Detective Word Leaping

give	green	large	grow
group	change		

Procedures

This section will take one week to cover. There will be instructor preparation time needed for making transparencies, the Buddy Partner Practice Sheet, and the Parent/Student Reading Together Coupon, pages 99-100. Follow the same daily procedures as were outlined in Unit IV, Section 1, pages 146–152. Go to Section 3.

Sight Word and Phonics Instruction: Rules 23 and 24

Instructor Background
Rule 23

Two *E*s together have the sound of long *E*, as in b<u>ee</u> and k<u>ee</u>p. This rule is consistently true. Emphasize memorizing the words and rule.

> ### Silly Story
>
> The twin vowels, EE were very loyal and helpful to each other. The other letters all knew they would always say the same sound they had agreed on. Always EE makes the sound of their name, long E.

Rule 24

The vowels *EA* together have more than one sound. They can have:

1. The long *E* sound *a lot of the time* as in r<u>ea</u>ch and s<u>ea</u>.

2. The short *E* sound some of the time as in h<u>ea</u>d and h<u>ea</u>vy.

3. The long *A* sound once in awhile as in gr<u>ea</u>t and br<u>ea</u>k.

4. The sound of *ER*, if the *R* is immediately after *EA* as in h<u>ear</u>d and l<u>ear</u>n.

There is no real rule to know when or why *EA* makes these sounds. The reader should first try the long sound of *E*. If that doesn't work, then use the words around it to help figure it out.

Silly Story

The vowels EA liked to pretend they were twins like the vowels EE. They even tried to make the same vowel sound of long E like the twins, EE. Most of the time they were able to say the long E sound, too.

But sometimes EA forgot they were pretending to be twins. When that happened they borrowed vowel Es short sound or vowel As long sound, and for no reason at all! Bossy R noticed this, so sometimes he got in behind EA and made them make his growling ER sound.

Emphasize learning all these words since it is hard to know what sound the *EA* will make.

New Sight Words

live	old	animal	any
most	very	boy	should

Detective Decoding Rule Search

three	need	great	mean
read	each	year	sleep

Detective Word Leaping

queen	keep	green	clean
tree	seem	feet	sea
head	real	eat	leave
near	earth	hear	learn
between			

Procedures

This section will take one week to cover. There will be instructor preparation time needed for making transparencies, the Buddy Partner Practice Sheet, and the Parent/Student Reading Together Coupon. pages 99-100. Follow the same daily procedures as were outlined in Unit IV, Section 1, pages 146 – 152. Go to Section 4.

Sight Word and Phonics Instruction: Rules 25 and 26

Instructor Background
Rule 25

The vowels *OO* together have the short *OO* sound as in sh<u>oo</u>k and b<u>oo</u>k, or the long *OO* sound as in z<u>oo</u> and p<u>oo</u>l.

Silly Story

Part I. What does an owl do best at night? You know, don't you? They can really <u>look</u> around and see well. The two letters OO noticed they looked just like the owl's big eyes, so wide open at night.

To show their respect to wise owl, the two letters OO decided that whenever they were together in a word they would make the sound heard in the middle of the word <u>look</u>, because owl loved to look around at night. Say the sound of OO that you hear in look—OO OO OO."

Silly Story, Part II

The two letters OO listened to the <u>hoot</u>ing sound the owl made as he watched all the night creatures <u>scoot</u>ing around at night. The two letters OO figured the owl must be talking when he <u>hoot</u>ed. Owl must say things like, "OO, see that mouse! OO, there goes a fox! The two letters OO decided they would make the OO, OO, OO, owl's excited OO sound, as their second sound.

Rule 26

The vowels *OI* at the beginning or in the middle of a word, and the letters *OY*, usually at the end of a word, usually have the sound of *OI* as in the words <u>oi</u>l, n<u>oi</u>se, and empl<u>oy</u>.

Silly Story

Whenever the letters O and I got together, in honor of their pet pig, they made the sound OI, because <u>oink</u> was the sound their pig made. Sometimes the OI got at the end of a word. Remember how lonely I was when it was at the end of a word? Remember the agreement I made earlier with Y?

Well, I asked O if it was OK for Y to help whenever O and I were together at the end of a word since I got so lonely there. "Absolutely OK," said O. "Y is a good friend to both of us." So when you see OI or OY together, they are honoring their pet pig and making the sound heard in <u>oink</u>.

New Sight Words

together	family	under	often	never
body	important	buy	pull	far

Detective Decoding Rule Search

look	too	good	soon	food
school	book	took	oil	point
boy				

Detective Word Leaping

noise	toy	voice	noise	shook
zoo	cook			

Procedures

These rules and words should be well learned. This section will take one week to cover. There will be instructor preparation time needed for making transparencies, the Buddy Partner Practice Sheet, and the Parent/Student Reading Together Coupon. Follow the same daily procedures as outlined in Unit IV, Section 1; at the appropriate time, add the following procedures.

Additional Procedures for Day One

1. Tell Silly Story Part I. Let the class watch as you draw a picture of two *O*s, then a large oval around the two *O*s. Next draw a beak, two tufted ears, feathers, a branch and claws around the branch. With a colored marker, outline around the two big *O*s (the owl's eyes). Put small eyeballs in the middle. Have the class say look, look, look to indicate what the owl's eyes do.

2. Tell Silly Story Part II. Have the students repeat the *OO* sound of the owl's hooting pleasure at what he is seeing at night.

3. Tell the Silly Story about *OI, OY*. Have the students repeat the *OI, OY* sound.

Additional Procedures for Day Two

1. On the transparency picture of the owl, add the letters *OO* on the right side and put eyeballs in them. Ask them to repeat the *OO* sound as in look.

2. Put the letters *OO* on the left side and ask the students to repeat the owl's excited *OO* sound as in hoot.

3. Put the letters *OI, OY* under the owl and ask the students to repeat the *OI, OY* sound as in <u>oi</u>nk.

4. As students review the Detective Decoding Rule Search transparency, have them tell you where each word should be written, under *OO* as in l<u>oo</u>k, *OO* as in h<u>oo</u>t or *OI, OY* as in <u>oi</u>nk. Write the words as they tell you.

Complete the lessons as given in Unit IV, Section 1, pages 146 - 152. Go to Section 5.

Sight Word and Phonics Instruction: Rule 27

Instructor Background
Rule 27

The vowels *OU* together have more than one sound. They can have:

1. *OW!* as in <u>ou</u>t and ab<u>ou</u>t.

2. Short *OO* as in c<u>ou</u>ld and w<u>ou</u>ld.

3. Long *OO* as in thr<u>ou</u>gh.

4. Short *O* as in th<u>ou</u>ght.

5. Short *U* as in y<u>ou</u>ng.

6. Long *O* as in th<u>ou</u>gh.

There is no way to know which sound *OU* will make in a word. The reader has to use the words around it to help figure out what the word says.

Silly Story

OU liked hearing the same Silly Stories you've been hearing. When deciding which sounds to copy, OU really wanted to be different. So OU chose to make <u>five</u> different sounds, more than any other letters. OU was the biggest Copy Cat of all the letters, and OU didn't get permission either!

OU copied the sound of OW who both took so much room when they were together, they often bumped into each other. Then they said, "Ow!"

OU copied OOs two sounds, because he liked the owl story. Remember the owl's eyes that would <u>look</u>? The two OOs used the sound like in <u>look</u>, oo, oo, oo. The OOs also used the sound of the owl's <u>hoot</u>, oo, oo, oo.

OU copied the short sound of O. Remember the Silly Story for short O? The round O shaped doughnut came out of the hot grease and said, "<u>Ah</u>, that feels good!"?

OU copied the short U sound. The umbrella handle looked like U, and also the word <u>u</u>mbrella started with the short sound of u, u, u.

OU now had copied five sounds, just like it meant to. Oh, oh, watch out! Here comes bossy R right behind OU, making OU say the same sound as the word OR.

That ought to make OU happy. Now OU has <u>six</u> different sounds. Wow! That <u>is</u> different. It doesn't use one sound much more than any other sound; and because OU likes being different, it wants the reader to use the words around it to figure out what sound its making.

New Sight Words

after	follow	mother	thing
answer	want	think	

Detective Decoding Rule Search

four	out	around	would
without	through	should	could
your	house	found	should

Detective Word Leaping

country	thought	sound	our
about	enough	mountain	young
round	around	group	

Procedures

All of these often used words should be learned well since they don't follow a consistent rule. This section will take one week to cover. There will be instructor preparation time needed for making transparencies, the Buddy Partner Practice Sheet, and the Parent/Student Reading Together Coupon, pages 97 to 100. Follow the same daily procedures as were outlined in Unit IV, Section 1, pages 146 to 152. Go to Section 6.

Sight Word and Phonics Instruction: Rules 28 and 29

Instructor Background
Rule 28

The consonant *N* immediately followed by *G*, often sounds like *N* and *G* are beginning to swallow their sounds as in si<u>ng</u> and sti<u>ng</u>.

Rule 29

The consonant *N* immediately followed by *K*, usually sounds like *N* is beginning to swallow its sound, while *K* has its own sound as in ta<u>nk</u> and ri<u>nk</u>.

Silly Story

Remember the unusual thing about G? When G follows N, they are both so shy, it sounds like N and G are both beginning to swallow their sounds like in the word si<u>ng</u>. Now say the word si<u>ng</u>. "Sing"

But let me tell you, K sure isn't shy when it follows N. K just goes right ahead and says its own sound while shy N still begins to swallow its sound like in the word thi<u>NK</u>. Now say the word thi<u>NK</u>. "Thi<u>nk</u>."

New Sight Words

study	different	letter	America	move
world	high	every	laugh	friend

Detective Decoding Rule Search
    long   along   young   song   thing
    think   long

Detective Word Leaping
    thank   sing   bring   drink   ring
    ink

Procedures

This rule is consistent most of the time. The rule and the words should be well learned. This section will take one week to cover. There will be instructor preparation time needed for making transparencies, the Buddy Partner Practice Sheet, and the Parent/Student Reading Together Coupon, pages 99 to 100. Follow the same daily procedures as were outlined in Unit IV, Section 1, pages 146 to 152. Go to Section 7.

Sight Word and Phonics Instruction: Rules 30 and 31

Instructor Background
Rule 30

The vowel *I* immediately followed by *LD* or *ND*, when the letters *ILD* or *IND* at the end of a one-syllable word, usually has the long *I* sound as in w<u>ild</u> and f<u>ind</u>.

Rule 31

The letters *IGH* usually have the long *I* sound as in h<u>igh</u> and l<u>igh</u>t.

Silly Story

Letter I liked its long sound better than its short sound. You see, the igloo that helped it remember its short sound also made I cold. So the letter I put up a big poster asking for letters to fill the job of helping it make its long sound more often.

Letters LD, ND, and GH immediately applied for the job. They all had the same idea. If they followed I, they could remind I to make its long sound, but most of the time they wanted to be at the end of a word.

Letter I hired them all. LD and ND insisted they wanted to also make their own sounds. Now whenever you see ILD or IND, especially at the end of a word, you know I will make its long sound and then the other letters will make their sounds.

GH, however, wanted to remain silent. When you see IGH, usually at the end of words, you will hear only the long I sound.

New Sight Words

| idea | until | don't | children | air |
| Indian | begin | above | because | open |

Detective Decoding Rule Search

| kind | find | might | right | high |
| light | night | | | |

Detective Word Leaping

| wild | child | sight |

Procedures

These rules and words should be well learned. This section will take one week to cover. There will be instructor preparation time needed for making transparencies, the Buddy Partner Practice Sheet, and the Parent/Student Reading Together Coupon, pages 99 to 100. Follow the same daily procedures as were outlined in Unit IV, Section 1, pages 146 to 152. Go to Section 8.

Sight Word and Phonics Instruction: Rules 6, 32, 33, and 34

Instructor Background
Rule 6

The two vowels *OW* often have the sound of *OW!* as in h<u>ow</u> and d<u>ow</u>n. Sometimes *OU* also has the sound of *OW!* as in h<u>ou</u>se.

Rule 32

The two vowels *OW* at the end of a short word usually have the long *O* sound as in sh<u>ow</u> and thr<u>ow</u>.

Rule 33

The vowel *O* immediately followed by *LD*, when the letters *OLD* at the end of a short word, usually has the long *O* sound as in h<u>old</u> and b<u>old</u>.

Silly Story

Remember the story about crowded OW and its OW! sound? Well, OW figured that if it was at the end of a word, it would have more room. Sure enough, when OW got to the end of the word, it had more room and a better view, too. "Oh, look at that view from the end of the word," OW said. From then on, when OW was at the end of a word,

---

it said, "<u>Oh</u>." LD thought it was so much fun following I, it would see if it could get a second job, following O to help it make its long sound. O liked the idea. Now OLD, usually found at the end of a word, makes the long O sound and then the sounds of the other letters.

Rule 34

When the vowels OA are together the O will almost always make its long sound, as in road.

Silly Story

O and A liked things to be simple. They thought it was great that when good friends EE, and good friends AI and AY were together they had just **one** sound that they always said. Do you remember? They had agreed that the first one got to say his name? Well, O and A couldn't get together very often, but they decided that when they **were** together O would say his name.

New Sight Words

example	never	both	law	sometimes
once	eye	river	paper	shall

Detective Decoding Rule Search

how	down	now	old	know	show
grow	low	sold	own	cold	hold
below					

Detective Decoding Rule Search 2

road	toad	coal	board	boat	coat
coast	soap	toast	roar	moat	goat

Detective Word Leaping

mold	fold	snow	yellow	follow	below
hoard	moat	coax	loathe	soar	

Procedures

These rules and words should be well learned. This section will take one week to cover. There will be instructor preparation time needed for making transparencies, the Buddy Partner Practice Sheet, and the Parent/Student Reading Together Coupon, pages 99 to 100. Follow the same daily procedures as were outlined in Unit IV, Section 1, pages 146 to 152. Go to Section 9.

Sight Word and Phonics Instruction: Rules 35, 36, 37, and 38

Instructor Background
Rule 35

The letters *AR* usually sound like the name of the letter *Rr* as in c<u>ar</u> and m<u>ar</u>ket.

Rule 36

The letters *WAR* usually have the sound as in <u>war</u>t and <u>war</u>m.

Rule 37

The vowels *WA*, if they are the only vowels in the word and not followed by an r, often have the sound as in <u>wa</u>nd, <u>wa</u>sp and <u>wa</u>sh.

Rule 38

The letters *WOR* usually have the sound as in <u>wor</u>ship and <u>wor</u>m.

Silly Story

Here comes Bossy R again, this time following vowel A, making the new sound AR, like you hear in c<u>ar</u>.

Did you know W sometimes played mischievous tricks, even on Bossy R? When W saw AR following it, W loved to change its sound to OR, like you hear in w<u>ar</u>. Whenever

W followed A in a word it tricked the A to say the short O sound like in the word wash. Oh, that mischievous W. Almost always when W saw OR following it, W used yet another trick. It changed OR into the sound of ER like in the word w<u>or</u>k. Do you think maybe W doesn't like to be followed by AR, A, or OR?

New Sight Words

upon	better	done	eight	saw
quiet	both	draw	seven	country

Detective Decoding Word Search

was	want	watch	water	word	car
work	hard	world	far	war	warm
wash	part	farther			

Procedures

These words should be well learned. This section will take one week to cover. There will be instructor preparation time needed for making transparencies, the Buddy Partner Practice Sheet, and the Parent/Student Reading Together Coupon, pages 99 to 100. Follow the same daily procedures as outlined in Unit IV, Section 1, pages 146 to 152. Go to Section 10.

Sight Word and Phonics Instruction: Rules 39, 40, 41, and 42

Instructor Background
Rule 39

The letters *GN* at the beginning of a word, usually have the sound of *N* and the *G* is silent as in <u>gn</u>aw and <u>gn</u>ome.

Rule 40

The letters *KN* at the beginning of a word, usually have the sound of *N* and the *K* is silent as in <u>kn</u>ow and <u>kn</u>ee.

Rule 41

The letters *WR* at the beginning of a word usually have the sound of *R* and the *W* is silent as in <u>wr</u>ite and <u>wr</u>ap.

Silly Story

The letters G and K were sometimes pushy to be first in line, especially if **N** was already there. N told G and K it didn't mind if they wanted to be first, but they couldn't be pushy and that G and K would have to be silent when they were in front of it. N would still be making its own N sound.

Remember mischievous W? Well, he saw G and K get away with being pushy in line, so he tried the same thing with the letter R. He pushed to be first in line, right in front of R. R told W it didn't mind, but W would have to be silent so R could make its own sound.

Rule 42

The vowels *AU* and *AW* usually have the short *O* sound as in p<u>au</u>se and t<u>au</u>ght, p<u>aw</u> and <u>shawl.</u>

Silly Story

Remember how W thought it would be fun if A, E, and O made some new sounds along with it? And how A, E, and O agreed that when one of them walked in front of W they <u>would</u> make a new sound with W. Remember that AW made the sound you hear in s<u>aw</u>?

AW said since AU wasn't in words very often, it could sometimes make the same sound as AW.

New Sight Words

almost	along	around	below	between	enough
farther	mountain	music	sentence	today	myself

Detective Decoding Rule Search

walk	draw	know	knee	sign	gnaw
write	wrap	wrong	saw	taught	draw
awful	law				

Procedures

These words should be learned well. This section will take one week to cover. There will be instructor preparation time needed for making transparencies, the Buddy Partner Practice Sheet, and the Parent/Student Reading Together Coupon, pages 99 to 100. Follow the same daily procedures as were outlined in Unit IV, Section 1, pages 146 to 152. Go to Section 11.

Blends Phonics Instruction: Rule 43

Instructor Background

These lessons will take two weeks to cover. The students will be practicing the blend sounds while reading new words using previously learned phonics rules.

Rule 43

If the two consonants together are ch, sh, th, ck, wh, ng, nk, ph, kn, gn, or wr, they make just one sound. But when other consonants are together in sets of two or three, their individual sounds will blend or smoosh together. They are bl, cl, pl, fl, gl, sl, br, cr, pr, fr, gr, dr, tr, sc, sk, sm, sn, sp, sw, st, squ, scr, str, spl, and spr. They will usually be at the beginning or middle of a word. The blends mp, nd, ft, nt, tch, and nch will usually be at the end of a word.

Silly Story

The consonants all liked to sing. Some of them had such close friends that they teamed together to make just one sound. You probably remember them and their sounds: ch, sh, th, ck, wh, ng, ph, kn, gn, and wr.

The rest of the time the consonants all (well, all but h and k) chose to keep their own individual sound. When they sang, you could hear their individual sounds, but they really like smooshing their sounds together. There are so many consonants, they could make lots of new sounds such as bl, cl, pl, fl, gl, sl, br, cr, pr, fr, gr, dr, tr, sc, sk, sm, sn, sp, sw, st, squ, scr, str, spl, spr, mp, nd, nk, ft, nt, tch, and nch. Lovely!

Blends at the Beginning of Words

BL

black	blame	blaze	bleach	blind
bloat	blood	bloom	blot	blow
blue	blunt			

CL

claim	clam	clap	class	clean
clear	clock	close	cloth	clothes
club	cloak			

PL

place	plain	plan	plug	plate
play	plead	pledge	plod	plead
plot	please			

FL

flag	flap	flame	floor	flare
flash	flea	flesh	flight	flit
float	flop	fly	flat	

GL

glad	glass	gleam	glide	gloom
glum	glean	glimpse	gloss	glow

SL

slack	slave	sleep	slight	slip
slide	slug	slot	slim	slime
slam	slope			

BR

brain	brand	brake	brisk	brave
bread	breath	bride	breeze	brew
bribe	brick	bridge	bright	bring

CR

crack	craft	crank	cream	crest
crew	cross	cram	cramp	croak
crust	crawl			

PR

prank	pray	praise	preach	pry
price	prince	print	prize	prompt
proof	prop			

FR

frail	frame	fraud	free	friend
fresh	fright	front	frost	froze
freeze	fret			

GR

ground	grab	gram	grand	grant
grape	graph	grasp	grass	gray
graze	grease	great	greed	green
greet	grid	grill		

DR

draft	drag	drain	drape	draw
dream	dress	drum	drift	drill
drink	drive			

TR

track	trail	train	trap	trash
treat	trench	tribe	trick	
truck	trust			

SC

scab	scarf	scar	scarc	scat
school	scorn	sculpt	scrimp	scam

SK

sketch	skin	ski	skill	skimp
skip	skunk	sky		

SM

smash	smoke	smooth	smudge	small
smell	smile	smack		

SN

snake	snug	snow	snare	snap
sneeze	snack	sneak		

SP

spoil	space	span	speak	spike
speed	spine	spice	spur	spite
spoon	sprout			

SW

swamp	swirl	sweep	sweet	swerve
swim	swoop	swam	swell	swift
swing				

ST

stag	stain	stairs	stale	stand
starch	starve	state	stove	steel
steal	steer	stick	stiff	stink
stir	stock	stone	stack	stool

SQU

squad	squid	squall	squat	square
squeak	squeeze	squirt	squash	squint

SCR

scrap	script	scrape	scratch	scram
screen	screw	scroll	scream	scrub

STR

straight	strange	straw	stream	strength
stride	string	stretch	strum	strap
strip	stripe	street	stream	strong

SPL

splash	splurge	splat	split	splendid

SPR

spring	spruce	sprang	sprain	sprawl
sprout	spry			

Blends at the End of Words

ST

fast	first	cast	nest	chest
mast	last	crust	must	test
list	just			

NK

bank	blank	sank	crank	plank
shrink	skunk	clank	slink	mink
sink	sank	rank	wink	

MP

jump	pump	camp	hump	stump
bump	lamp	ramp	stamp	mumps
cramp	chimp	clump	clamp	plump

ND

hand	land	stand	rind	kind
mind	found	round		

FT

left	drift	draft	craft	raft
shaft	left	shift		

NT

sent	spent	bent	lent	want
front	font	flint	plant	went

TCH and NCH

pitch	witch	snitch	patch	flinch
pinch				

Procedures for Day One

1. Tell the Silly Story.

2. Tell the students that there are fewer consonant combinations that make just one sound when they are together, and that they already recognize them.

3. Review the consonants that when together make only one sound: ch, sh, th, ck, wh, ng, ph, kn, gn, wr. (See pages 69-75 and 175-176.) Be sure the students know these letter combinations make only one sound. Blends make the sound of both letters.

Procedures for Day Two

1. Retell the "Silly Story".
2. Display the transparencies with words the bl, cl, pl, fl, gl, and sl words. Have the students identify where the blends are located.
3. Underline each blend and say the each word, smooshing the letter sounds in the blend together

Procedures for Day Three

1. Retell the "Silly Story".
2. Display the transparencies with the br. cr. pr, fr. gr. dr. and tr words.
3. Have the students identify where the blends are located in each word.   4. Underline each blend and say each word, smooshing the letter sounds in the blends together.

Procedures for Day Four

1. Partner the students together.
2. Give them papers with Day Two and Day Three with the blend words listed on them. Ask the partners to review them by reading them to each other, helping as needed.
3. Ask them to take the papers home and read the words to a parent or another adult.

Procedures for Day Five

Play the Memory and/or Puff game using the words from Day Two and Day Three.

Procedures for Day Six

1. Display the transparencies with the sc, sk, sm, sn, sp, sw, and st words.
2. Have the students identify the blends.
3. Have the students identify where the blends are located in each word.
4. Underline each blend and say each word, smooshing the letter sounds in the blends together.

Procedures for Day Seven

1. Display the transparencies with the squ, scr, str, spl, and spr words.
2. Have the students identify the blends, noticing that there are three letters in each blend and that each letter still says its own sound.
3. Have the students identify where the blends are located in each word.
4. Underline each blend and say each word, smooshing the letter sounds in the blends together.

Procedures for Day Eight

1. Display the transparencies with the st, nk, mp, nt, ft, pt, nt, tch and nch words.
2. Have the students identify where the blends are located in each word.
3. Underline each blend and say each word, smooshing the letter sounds in the blends together.

Procedures for Day Nine

1. Partner the students together.
2. Give them papers with Day One, Day Two and Day Three with the blend words listed on them.
3. Ask them to review them by reading them to each other, helping as needed.
4. Ask them to take the papers home and read the words to someone else.

Procedures for Day Ten

Play the Memory and/or Puff game using the words from Day Six, Day Seven and Day Eight.

These sessions have given your student practice in using previously learned rules. He can now confidently figure out unknown words by decoding. Give him lots of praise in his ability to apply the rules he worked so hard to learn. Verbally and visually experience his excitement. Go on to Unit V, Section 1.

UNIT V

DECODING LONGER WORDS USING SYLLABLE RULES, MORE SUFFIXES, COMPOUND WORDS, AND CONTRACTIONS

Sight Word and Syllable Instruction: Rules 44, 45, 46, and 47

Instructor Background

This section will take one week to cover. There will be instructor preparation time needed for making transparencies, the Buddy Partner Practice Sheets, and the Parent/Student Reading Together Coupon.

A syllable is a <u>word part</u> that contains one <u>vowel sound</u>. Each <u>vowel sound</u> in a word is called a <u>vowel unit</u>. See the word formula below.

syllable = word part = vowel sound = vowel unit = syllable

Rule 44

Each syllable has one vowel sound.

Rule 45

When *Y* is at the end of a longer word of two or more syllables, Y has the sound of long *E*. *Y* becomes a syllable along with the consonants in front of it OR a syllable of its own.

Silly Story

Y really liked being uncrowded at the end of words, but when the words got longer, Y felt scared, like it was hanging over a cliff. "EEEE!" Y cried out <u>every</u> time. After awhile Y became more used to hanging on the end of a longer word, but from habit Y still cried out "EEEE". Vowel E said that it was fine for Y to use its sound when it was hanging from the end of a longer word.

Rule 46

If there are two consonants together between vowel sounds and they don't have to stay together to make one sound, the word usually divides between them.

Rule 47

If there is only one consonant between the vowel units, usually the word divides in front of the consonant. The vowel in the front has its long sound. If the word doesn't sound right, divide the word behind the consonant. The vowel in front of the consonant now has a short sound.

Sample Words to Show Vowel Units and Syllables

For the instructor, the following words will help show vowel units and syllables. The <u>vowel unit</u> is underlined.

h <u>o</u> m e

The vowel <u>sound</u> heard is long *o*, made by an *o* and silent *e*. The letter *o* is called a vowel unit. The silent vowel *e* at the end makes no sound, so it is not a vowel unit. Since the word has one vowel unit, the word has <u>one syllable</u>.

r <u>u</u> n

The vowel <u>sound</u> heard is short *u*, made by the letter *u*. The letter *u* is called a vowel unit. Since the word has one vowel unit, the word has <u>one syllable</u>.

r <u>a i</u> n

The vowel <u>sound</u> heard is long *a*, made by the letters *ai*. The vowel unit consists of the letters *ai*. Since the word has one vowel unit, the word has <u>one syllable</u>.

h <u>o w</u>

The vowel <u>sound</u> heard is *ow*, made by the letters *ow*. The vowel unit consists of the letters *ow*. Since the word has one vowel unit, the word has <u>one syllable</u>.

c <u>a r</u> r <u>y</u>

The vowel <u>sounds</u> heard are *air* and long *e*, made by the letters *ar* and *y*. The letters *ar* are a vowel unit and the letter *y* at the end of the word is a vowel unit. Since the word has two vowel units, the word has <u>two syllables</u>.

f <u>a</u> m <u>i</u> l <u>y</u>

The vowel <u>sounds</u> heard are short *a*, short *i* and long *e*. The letter *a* makes the sound of short *a*, the letter *i* makes the sound of short *i*, and the letter *y* at the end of the word makes the sound of long *e*. The vowel units are the letters *a*, *i*, and *y*. Since the word has three vowel units, the word has <u>three syllables</u>.

f r <u>y</u>

The vowel <u>sound</u> heard is long *i*, made by the *y* at the end of the word. The letter *y* becomes a vowel unit. Since the word has only one vowel unit, the word has <u>one syllable</u>.

New Sight Words

baby	they	way	funny	today
many				

Detective Decoding Rule Search

body	only	every	country	family
story	carry	study	any	cry
play	say	fly	try	why
any	boy	buy	toy	away

—189—

More Words for Syllable Lessons

Part One		Part Two		
almost	along	around	sentence	second
seven	farther	between	friends	mountain
because	below	opening	music	landing
picture	paper	together	under	until
without	yellow	after	again	watered
America	animal	another	answer	letter
different	example	follow	watermelon	
Indian	important	number		

Procedures for Day One

1. With the students quickly review the more difficult words previously taught, using the Sight Word Practice overhead transparency.

2. Display the New Sight Words transparency. Teach as in earlier sessions.

3. Display the Detective Rule Search transparency.

4. Ask students to discover any new rule or previously learned rules. Using a temporary overhead marker, write the rule(s) when the students discover it.

5. Suggest they check to see if your rule(s) work(s) with all the words. Wording for the rule doesn't have to be the same if the wording has the same meaning. Go through each word, having students say it along with you. After each word, solicit student help, such as "Where was the *Y* in each word? What sound did the *Y* make in each word? Was *Y* the only vowel sound in the word? What other vowel sound(s) did you hear?"

6. Say, "Let's say the words together and see if we were good detectives, if we found the rule. In short words did the *Y* at the end of the word make a long *I* sound? In long words did the *Y* at the end of the word always make a long *E* sound?" When and why did the *Y* follow a different rule. Write each word in a Short Words or Long Words column as the students repeat each word again and tell which column to write it in.

7. Ask the students what is alike about the short words. Y *was the only vowel sound heard in the word.* Ask the students what is

alike about the long words. Y *was not the only vowel sound (unit) heard in the word.*

8. If the students didn't find the correct rule, repeat the procedure until the correct rule is found.

9. Tell the Silly Story about *Y* and its new rule. They may want to recall some of the other Silly Stories about *Y* and its rules.

10. Have the students read the words without your help, as you use the sweeping finger. Ask one or more student volunteers to be the instructors for this step.

Procedures for Day Two

1. Display the Sight Word Practice and New Sight Words transparencies. Go over them with as much speed or deliberation as the students need.

2. Display the Detective Decoding Rule Search transparency with day one's list of short and longer words. Review the rule(s) they discovered and repeat the words several times in different ways.

3. Using the short word list, ask what vowel sound they <u>heard</u>; underline the *Y* and put the sound heard above it.

4. Using the long word list, after saying each word, ask what vowel sound(s) they heard; underline each vowel unit and put a symbol above it to indicate the sound.

5. Repeat the first word on the long word list. Ask them how many vowel sounds were in it. Write the number beside the word. Tell them that each <u>vowel</u> <u>sound</u> they heard is called a <u>vowel unit</u>. Ask how many vowel units were in the word.

6. Go through the rest of the words, determining how many vowel units are in each word, writing the number beside the word.

7. Read the words again, emphasizing the vowel units.

8. *If instructing a group:* Buddy partner the students using the Buddy Partner Chart. Remind them that each buddy is responsible to help his/her partner successfully read the Buddy Partner Practice Sheet. You will become partners in case of absences. If a student needs considerable additional assistance, you may sit with the partners or work individually with the student. When completed, have the students return the Practice Partner Sheet to you.

If instructing an individual: You and the student are always buddy partners, reading the Buddy Partner Practice Sheet together. As the students buddy partner practice reading to each other, you will oversee, assist, and note items that need reteaching.

Procedures for Day Three

1. Display the New Sight Words transparency and quickly go through them.
2. Display a transparency of Part One, More Words for Syllable Lessons.
3. Go through the first four words, underlining each vowel unit and writing the number of vowel units beside the word.
4. Explain that each vowel unit is also a syllable. Ask how many syllables are in each of the first four words.
5. Repeat with all the other words.
6. Provide students with buddy partner practice time and his/her weekly Buddy Partner Practice Sheet.
7. Have the students return the Buddy Practice Partner Sheet to you.

Procedures for Day Four

1. Display the New Sight Words transparency and quickly go through them.
2. Display Part Two, More Words for Syllable Lessons. Read the words again, asking the students to clap on each vowel sound/unit or syllable.
3. Go through each word, underlining each vowel unit, writing the number of vowel units, called syllables, beside the words.
4. Provide buddy partner practice time using the same sheet as on the second and third days.
5. Have the students return the Buddy Practice Partner Sheet to you.
6. Provide fifteen to twenty minutes of independent reading time for the students, as well as reading games and activities.

Procedures for Day Five

1. Provide students with the Buddy Partner Practice Sheet with the Parent/Student Reading Together Coupon attached. Have each student write his/her name on the Parent/Student Reading Together Coupon.

   If instructing an individual: Listen to the student read to you while you evaluate. Send home the packet with the Buddy Partner Practice Sheets and the Parent/Student Reading Together Coupon.

   If instructing a group: Have buddy partners read the Buddy Partner Practice sheet to each other making sure each is reading successfully. When the buddy partners finish working with each other, they put their papers in a specific basket and begin independent silent reading using the classroom library. Listen to each set of buddy partners read their Buddy Partner Practice Sheets. Have the partners return to silent reading while you continue to evaluate other students' progress. Send home the homework Packet with the Buddy Partner Practice Sheets and the Parent/Student Reading Together Coupon. Remind the students when they are due.

Go to Section 2.

Suffix Instruction: Rules 10 Through 18, 48 Through 50

Instructor Background

This section will take one week to cover. There will be instructor preparation time needed for making transparencies, the Buddy Partner Practice Sheets, and the Parent/Student Reading Together Coupon.

By adding the common suffixes of *S, ES, ED,* and *ING* to sight words learned in Unit IV, Sections 1 through 10, students will review suffixes and sight words while learning new words.

When adding a suffix, the original word is called a <u>base or root word</u>. Use both terms so the student is familiar with both.

The charts that include the base words with the suffixes are for the instructor's reference. The charts with only the base words are for the instructors to copy onto a transparency.

Rule 10

Most of the time, just add the suffix if a short base word ends with two consonants, two vowels or two vowels before a single consonant as in walk<u>ed</u>, show<u>s</u> and load<u>ing</u>.

Rule 11

Suffix *S* has the <u>sound</u> of the letter *S* as in number<u>s</u> and play<u>s</u>. It is not a syllable.

Rule 12

The suffix *ES* may be added to a base word that ends with the voiceless sound of *O, S, SH, CH,* or *J* as in bush<u>es</u> and wish<u>es</u>. The *ES* sounds like the letter *Ss* <u>name</u> except when it follows *O*. Then *ES* has the <u>sound</u> of the letter *S*. Suffix *ES* is usually a syllable.

Rule 13

Suffix *ED* is added to a base word that ends with a vowel or voiced consonant sound. The suffix *ED* then has the *D* sound as in play<u>ed</u>, fill<u>ed</u>, and lean<u>ed</u>. This is the way the suffix *ED* is used most of the time. It is not a syllable.

Rule 14

Suffix *ED* is added to a base word that ends with a voiceless consonant sound. The suffix *ED* then has the *T* sound as in help<u>ed</u>, look<u>ed</u>, and wish<u>ed</u>. This is the way the suffix *ED* is used some of the time. It is not a syllable.

Rule 15

Suffix *ED* is added to a base word that ends with the *D* or *T* sound. The suffix *ED* then sounds like the boy's name, Ed, as in want<u>ed</u>, shout<u>ed</u>, and load<u>ed</u>. This is the way the suffix *ED* is used the least. It is a syllable.

Rule 16

Suffix *ING* has the sound as in start<u>ing</u> and bark<u>ing</u>. Suffix *ING* is a syllable.

Rule 17

Silent *E* is removed from the end of a base word if a suffix with a vowel at the beginning is added as in lin<u>ed</u> and fil<u>ing</u>.

Silly Story

Remember when E is at the end of a word, it likes being the only vowel there and doesn't want another vowel to join it at the end of a word? E wants to rest silently, and it doesn't want to change its sound.

> When suffix ES, ED, ING, EST or ER comes to join E at the end of a word, that puts another vowel, E, next to E. E just wants to rest silently, not to change its sound, so E usually just quietly drops and goes away.
>
> Sometimes LY or FUL comes to the end of a word to join E. To have a consonant next to E was just fine, so E often stayed with LY and FUL.

Rule 18

Silent E sometimes has two jobs at the end of a base word. It may indicate the vowel in the middle has a long vowel sound and that *C* or *G* has a soft sound as in pag<u>ed</u> and fac<u>es</u>.

Procedures for Day One

1. With a sheet of paper, cover the transparency Suffix Magic Chart C-1 from the headings down.

2. Review definitions of a base and/or root word and a suffix and suffix sounds.

3. Tell the students they will not be detectives today, but will be the magicians, to please put on their magician's hat and be ready to change a base word they already know into new words.

4. Move the sheet of paper below the first word. Ask the students to use magic with suffix *S* and *ES* and the base word to make a new word. When the students read the new word, ask the students to spell the new word. Write it in the column. Most likely they will not spell it correctly. Tell them you forgot something! The wizard told you a Silly Story about Silent *E* to tell his magicians.

5. Tell the Silly Story.

6. Ask the students to try magic again, that this is harder magic. Write the word as it is spelled. Do the same with suffix *ED* and suffix *ING*. Not all words will use all the suffixes.

7. Continue across the transparency in the same manner. Follow the same procedure with suffix *ED* and suffix *ING*. Not all words will use all the suffixes.

Suffix Magic Chart C

Base Words	Suffix s or es	Suffix ed	Suffix ing
place	places	placed	placing
little			
live	lives	lived	living
give	gives		giving
name	names	named	naming
large			
move	moves	moved	moving
picture	pictures	pictured	picturing
change	changes	changed	changing
house	houses	housed	housing
page	pages	paged	paging
eye	eyes	eyed	eyeing
close	closes	closed	closing
close			
state	states	stated	stating
state			
late			

Suffix Magic Chart C-1

Base Words	Suffix s or es	Suffix ed	Suffix ing
place			
little			
live			
give			
name			
large			
move			
picture			
change			
house			
page			
eye			
close			
close			
state			
state			
late			

8. Have the "magician(s)" read across the rows along with you. First read the base word and then the newly created "magic" words. Have fun along with them.

9. Ask the students what was alike about all the base words and what happened when a suffix was added.

10. Have the students buddy partner practice using a Buddy Partner Practice Sheet duplicated from the transparencies.

Procedures for Day Two

1. Display overhead transparency, Suffix Magic Chart D-1. With a sheet of paper, cover the transparency from the headings down.

2. Solicit the student's help to explain about base words, suffixes, and suffix sounds.

3. Tell the students to be magicians again, to please put on the magician's hat and be ready to use the strongest magic on the base words.

4. Move the sheet of paper below the first word. Ask the students to use magic with *S* or *ES* and the base word to make a new word. When the students read the new word, ask how to spell it. Write the word under the suffix *S* or *ES* column. Do the same with suffix *ED* and suffix *ING*. Not all words will use all the suffixes.

5. Ask what the students found alike about all the base words. Help as needed.

6. Together read each row to make sure the suffix rule worked.

7. Have the students buddy partner practice using a Buddy Partner Practice Sheet duplicated from the transparencies.

Procedures for Day Three

1. Display overhead transparency, Suffix Magic Chart E-1. With a sheet of paper cover the transparency from the headings down.

2. Solicit the students help to explain about base words, suffixes, and suffix sounds.

3. Tell the students to be magicians again, to please put on the magician's hat and be ready to use the strongest magic on the base words.

4. Move the sheet of paper below the first word. Ask the students to use magic with *S, ES*, and the base word to make a new word.

Suffix Magic Chart D

Base Words	Suffix s or es	Suffix ed	Suffix ing
sound	sounds	sounded	sounding
end	ends	ended	ending
kind			
kind	kinds		
hand	hands	handed	handing
hand	hands		
work	works	worked	working
read	reads		reading
back	backs	backed	backing
think	thinks		thinking
year	years		
most			
help	helps	helped	helping
right	rights		
right	rights	righted	righting
mean	means		
mean			

Suffix Magic Chart D-1

Base Words	Suffix s or es	Suffix ed	Suffix ing
sound			
end			
kind			
kind			
hand			
hand			
work			
read			
back			
think			
year			
most			
help			
right			
right			
mean			
mean			

When the students read the new word, ask how to spell it. Write the word under the suffix *S/ES* column. Do the same with suffix *ED* and suffix *ING*. Not all words will use all the suffixes.

5. Ask what the students noticed what was alike about all the base words. See if the students can figure out the suffix rule. Help as needed.

6. Together read each row to make sure the suffix rule worked.

7. Have the students buddy partner practice using a Buddy Partner Practice Sheet duplicated from the transparencies.

Procedures for Day Four

1. Solicit the students help to explain base words, suffixes, and suffix sounds.

2. Display overhead transparency, Suffix Magic F-1, then G-1. With a sheet of paper cover the transparency from the headings down.

3. Tell the students to be magicians again, to please put on the magician's hat and be ready to use the strongest magic on the base words.

4. Move the sheet of paper below the first word. Ask the students to use magic with *S*, *ES*, and the base word to make a new word. When the students read the new word, ask them how to spell it. Write the word under the suffix *S/ES* column. Do the same with suffix *ED* and suffix *ING*. Not all words will use all the suffixes.

5. Ask what was noticed that was alike about all the base words. See if the students can figure out the suffix rules. Help as needed.

6. Together read each row to make sure the suffix rules worked.

7. Have the students buddy partner practice using a Buddy Practice Sheet duplicated from the transparencies.

Suffix Magic Chart E

Base Words	Suffix s or es	Suffix ed	Suffix ing
follow	follows	followed	following
show	shows	showed	showing
show	shows		
want	wants	wanted	wanting
form	forms	formed	forming
small			
even	evens	evened	evening
turn	turns	turned	turning
turn	turns		
ask	asks	asked	asking
know	knows		knowing
land	lands	landed	landing
land	lands		
different			
spell	spells	spelled	spelling
point	points	pointed	pointing

Suffix Magic Chart E-1

Base Words	Suffix s or es	Suffix ed	Suffix ing
follow			
show			
show			
want			
form			
small			
even			
turn			
turn			
ask			
know			
land			
land			
different			
spell			
point			

Suffix Magic Chart F

Base Words	Suffix s or es	Suffix ed	Suffix ing
learn	learns	learned	learning
word	words	worded	wording
near	nears	neared	nearing
add	adds	added	adding
plant	plants	planted	planting
school	schools	schooled	schooling
keep	keeps		keeping
start	starts	started	starting
light	lights		lighting
light	lights		
thought	thoughts		
head	heads	headed	
head	heads	headed	heading
hard			
open	opens	opened	opening
paper	papers		
paper	papers	papered	papering

Suffix Magic Chart F-1

Base Words	Suffix s or es	Suffix ed	Suffix ing
learn			
word			
near			
add			
plant			
school			
keep			
start			
light			
light			
thought			
head			
head			
hard			
open			
paper			
paper			

Suffix Magic Chart G

Base Words	Suffix s or es	Suffix ed	Suffix ing
grow	grows		growing
miss	misses	missed	missing
watch	watches	watched	watching
young			
color	colors	colored	coloring
color	colors		
clean			
full			
old			
tell	tells		telling
answer	answers	answered	answering
group	groups	grouped	grouping
night	nights		
walk	walks	walked	walking

Suffix Magic Chart G-1

Base Words	Suffix s or es	Suffix ed	Suffix ing
grow			
miss			
watch			
young			
color			
color			
clean			
full			
old			
tell			
answer			
group			
night			
walk			

Instructor Background for Day Five
Rule 48

If there is only one consonant at the end of a one syllable base word, usually the consonant is doubled before adding any suffix except *S*, as in cut<u>ting</u> and hop<u>ped</u>.

Silly Story

The base words that had one vowel in the middle and ended with one consonant had a very serious meeting. They didn't know how to protect their vowel. They moaned, "If the suffix is removed, E will get in there real fast to hop over the one consonant and make the vowel say its name. <u>That</u> would change <u>us</u> into a different base word!"

"We know what to do," volunteered the consonants at the word ends.

"We'll just double ourselves when a suffix is added. E can't jump over two consonants, so he won't get in there real fast. After E has given up, we can un-double ourselves. You base words will be safe then."

And that is why a single ending consonant sometimes doubles itself before a suffix is added.

Rule 49

If *Y* immediately follows a consonant at the end of a two syllable base word, and the suffix does not begin with *I*, change the *Y* to *I* when the suffix is added as in bab<u>i</u>es and sill<u>i</u>est.

Silly Story

Remember how Y likes to be at the end of a word. When a suffix joins a base word, Y calls for I to come, that it is feeling very crowded now that it's no longer at the end of the word. I comes bouncing right along to take its place in the middle of the word.

Once in awhile I is at the beginning of the suffix, so Y has to stay in the word. At least I is right there with Y trying to make Y feel better.

Rule 50

If the base word ends with the vowels *AY, OY,* or *UY,* the *Y* is not changed to *I* before a suffix is added as in pl<u>ay</u>*ed,* to<u>y</u>*s,* and bu<u>y</u>*ing.*

Silly Story

Y is really a very important letter with so many jobs to do. Sometimes he makes a sound with AY, OY, or UY. Usually Y is with those letters at the end of a word.

When a suffix comes to join a word where AY, OY, or UY are at the end, Y doesn't leave. Y just grits his teeth and sticks with his friends. Otherwise their sounds would change, and he would feel terrible.

Procedures for Day Five

Today's lessons will include review and the new rules above.

1. Solicit the students help to explain base words, suffixes and suffix sounds.

2. Display overhead transparency, Suffix Magic Chart H-1. With a sheet of paper cover the transparency from the headings down.

3. Tell the students to be a magician again, to please put on the magician's hat and be ready to use their strongest magic on the base words.

4. Move the sheet of paper below the first word. Ask them to use their magic with *S, ES,* and the base word to make a new word. When they say the new word, ask them how to spell it. Write the word under the suffix *S/ES* column.

5. With suffix *ED* and suffix *ING* spelling will probably not double the letters. Have the students observe that in each word there is only one consonant between the vowel in the middle and the suffix. Ask them what that tells them about the vowel in the middle.

(It will have a long sound.) Tell the Silly Story. Not all words will use all the suffixes.

6. Ask what they should do to the *ED* and *ING* words. *Double the consonant.* Have them spell the words. Have the students state in their own words Rule 46. Help as needed.

7. Together read each row to make sure the suffix rules worked.

8. Display Chart I-1. Ask the students what is alike about each word.

9. Have them spell the words with suffixes. They may notice that the Y at the end is a vowel, so they can't add a suffix that begins with a vowel.

10. Tell the Silly Story.

11. Have the students correct the spellings. Remind them of Rule 30, that when two vowels are at the end of the word, the suffix is simply added.

12. Have the students state a rule for *Y* at the end of the word when a suffix is added.

13. Together read each row to make sure the suffix rules worked.

14. Staple all Buddy Partner Practice Sheets together, including the current day's, and a Parent/Student Homework Coupon. Have the students write their name on the coupon.

15. *If instructing a group:* Have the students buddy partner practice, then read silently a book of their choice. Listen to each set of buddy partners read their Buddy Partner Practice Sheets. Select words randomly from the packet for the partners to read. Check the basic understanding and record what needs review later. Write a positive note on each students Buddy Partner Practice Sheet.

16. Have the partners return to silent reading while you continue to evaluate other students' progress.

17. Students take the Parent/Student Reading Together Coupon packet home to go over with parents and return the following week.

Go to Section 3.

Suffix Magic Chart H

Base Words	Suffix s or es	Suffix ed	Suffix ing
begin	begins		beginning
stop	stops	stopped	stopping
cut	cuts		cutting
hot			
wet	wets	wetted	wetting

Suffix Magic Chart H-1

Base Words	Suffix s or es	Suffix ed	Suffix ing
begin			
stop			
cut			
hot			
wet			

Suffix Magic Chart I

Base Words	Suffix s or es	Suffix ed	Suffix ing
study	studies	studied	studying
city	cities		
story	stories		
carry	carries	carried	carrying
play	plays	played	playing
boy	boys		
buy	buys		buying

Suffix Magic Chart I-1

Base Words	Suffix s or es	Suffix ed	Suffix ing
study			
city			
story			
carry			
play			
boy			
buy			

Suffix Review and Instruction: Rules 51 Through 54

Instructor Background

This section will take one week to cover. There will be instructor preparation time needed for making transparencies, the Buddy Partner Practice Sheets, the Parent/Student Reading Together Coupon, and a game.

By adding the common suffixes of *EST, ER, LY,* and *FUL* to the sight words in Unit V, Section 1, the student will review suffixes and sight words while learning new words.

When adding a suffix, the original word is called a *base* or *root word.* Use both terms so the student is familiar with both.

The charts that include the base words with the suffixes are for the instructor's reference. The charts that have only the base words are for the instructor to copy onto a transparency.

For review, refer to Appendix G, Rules 10 through 18 and 48 through 54.

Rule 51

The suffix *EST* is a syllable. It has the short *E* sound, as in larg<u>est</u> and happi<u>est</u>.

Rule 52

Suffix *ER* is a syllable and has the sound as in read<u>er</u> and bak<u>er</u>.

Rule 53

Suffix *LY* is a syllable. It has the sound as in name<u>ly</u> and close<u>ly</u>.

Rule 54

Suffix *FUL* is a syllable. Suffix *FUL* has the sound as in cup<u>ful</u> and bucket<u>ful</u>.

Procedures for Day One

1. With a sheet of paper, cover the transparency Suffix Magic Chart J-1 from the headings down.

2. Move the sheet of paper below the first word. Ask the students to use magic with the suffix *EST* and the base word to make a new word. When the students read the new word, ask the students to spell the new word. Write it in the column. One hopes the students will remember the silent *E* rule and spell it correctly. Ask the students to remind you of the story. Tell them there's even more.

Silly Story

Remember when E is at the end of a word, it likes being the only vowel there and doesn't want another vowel to join it at the end of a word? E wants to rest silently, and it doesn't want to change its sound.

When suffix EST or ER comes to join E at the end of a word, that puts another vowel, E, next to E. E just wants to rest silently, not to change its sound, so E usually just quietly drops and goes away.

Sometimes LY or FUL comes to the end of a word to join E. To have a consonant next to E is just fine, so E stayed with LY and FUL.

3. Continue across the transparency in the same manner. Follow the same procedure with suffix *ER*, suffix *LY*, and suffix *FUL*. Not all words will use all the suffixes.

Suffix Magic Chart J

Base Word	Suffix est	Suffix er	Suffix ly	Suffix ful
place		placer		
little	littlest	littler		
live				
give		giver		
name		namer	namely	
large	largest	larger	largely	
move		mover		
picture		picturer		
change		changer		
house				
page		pager		
eye		eyer		
close		closer		
close	closest	closer	closely	
state		stater		
state			stately	
late	latest		lately	

Suffix Magic Chart J-1

Base Word	Suffix est	Suffix er	Suffix ly	Suffix ful
place				
little				
live				
give				
name				
large				
move				
picture				
change				
house				
page				
eye				
close				
close				
state				
state				
late				

4. Have the "magician(s)" read across the rows along with you. Read the base word first and then the newly created "magic" words. Have fun along with them.

5. Ask the students what was alike about all the base words and what happened when a suffix was added.

6. Have the students buddy partner practice using a Buddy Partner Practice Sheet duplicated from the transparencies.

Procedures for Day Two

1. Display the overhead transparency, Suffix Magic Chart K-1. With a sheet of paper, cover the transparency from the headings down.

2. Solicit the students' help to explain about base words, suffixes, and suffix sounds.

3. Tell the students to be magicians again, to please put on the magician's hat and be ready to use the strongest magic on the base words.

4. Move the sheet of paper below the first word. Ask the students to use magic with *EST* and the base word to make a new word. When the students read the new word, ask how to spell it. Write the word under the suffix *EST* column. Do the same with suffix *ER*, suffix *LY,* and suffix *FUL*. Not all words will use all suffixes.

5. Ask the students what they noticed that was alike about all the base words. Have them recall the suffix rule. Help as needed.

6. Together, read each row to make sure the suffix rule worked.

7. Have the students buddy partner practice using a Buddy Partner Practice Sheet duplicated from the transparencies.

Procedures for Day Three

Follow day two's procedures using Chart L-1.

Procedures for Day Four

Follow day two's procedures using Charts M-1 and N-1.

Procedures for Day Five

1. Follow day two's procedures using Charts O-1 and P-1.

2. Staple all Buddy Partner Practice Sheets together, including the

current day's, and a Parent/Student Reading Together Coupon. Have the students write their name on the coupon. Allow time for buddy partner practice.

3. When buddy partners finish working, they should put their papers in a specific basket and begin independent silent reading, using the classroom library.

4. *If instructing a group:* Listen to each set of buddy partners read their Buddy Partner Practice Sheets. Select words randomly from the packet for the partners to read. Check the basic understanding and record what needs later review. Write a positive note on the Buddy Partner Practice Sheet.

Students take the Parent/Student Reading Together Coupon packet home to go over with parents and return the following week.

Play the game Wizard's Brew as directed in Unit IV, Section 1. If necessary, have the students begin to play the game with you so they can relearn it. Once the game is understood, have the students play in groups of three to six.

If tutoring a single student, play with the student.

Suffix Magic Chart K

Base Word	Suffix est	Suffix er	Suffix ly	Suffix ful
sound	soundest	sounder	soundly	
end				
kind	kindest	kinder	kindly	
kind				
hand		hander		
hand				handful
work		worker		
read		reader		
back		backer		
think		thinker		
year			yearly	
most			mostly	
help		helper		
right			rightly	rightful
right		righter		
mean				
mean	meanest	meaner	meanly	

Suffix Magic Chart K-1

Base Word	Suffix est	Suffix er	Suffix ly	Suffix ful
sound				
end				
kind				
kind				
hand				
hand				
work				
read				
back				
think				
year				
most				
help				
right				
right				
mean				
mean				

Suffix Magic Chart L

Base Word	Suffix est	Suffix er	Suffix ly	Suffix ful
follow		follower		
show		shower		
show				
want				
form		former		
small	smallest	smaller		
even	evenest	evener	evenly	
turn		turner		
ask				
ask		asker		
know				
read				
land				
land				
different			differently	
spell		speller		
point		pointer		

Suffix Magic Chart L-1

Base Word	Suffix est	Suffix er	Suffix ly	Suffix ful
follow				
show				
show				
want				
form				
small				
even				
turn				
ask				
ask				
know				
read				
land				
land				
different				
spell				
point				

Suffix Magic Chart M

Base Word	Suffix est	Suffix er	Suffix ly	Suffix ful
learn		learner		
word		worder		
near	nearest	nearer	nearly	
add		adder		
plant		planter		
school				
keep		keeper		
start		starter		
light	lightest	lighter		
light			lightly	
thought				thoughtful
head				
head				
hard	hardest	harder	hardly	
open		opener	openly	
paper				
paper		papered		

Suffix Magic Chart M-1

Base Word	Suffix est	Suffix er	Suffix ly	Suffix ful
learn				
word				
near				
add				
plant				
school				
keep				
start				
light				
light				
thought				
head				
head				
hard				
open				
paper				
paper				

Suffix Magic Chart N

Base Word	Suffix est	Suffix er	Suffix ly	Suffix ful
grow		grower		
miss		misser		
watch		watcher		watchful
young	youngest	younger		
color		colorer		
color				colorful
clean	cleanest	cleaner		
old	oldest	older		
full	fullest	fuller	fully	
tell		teller		
answer		answerer		
group				
night			nightly	
walk		walker		

Suffix Magic Chart N-1

Base Word	Suffix est	Suffix er	Suffix ly	Suffix ful
grow				
miss				
watch				
young				
color				
color				
clean				
old				
full				
tell				
answer				
group				
night				
walk				

Suffix Magic Chart O

Base Word	Suffix est	Suffix er	Suffix ly	Suffix ful
begin		beginner		
stop		stopper		
cut		cutter		
hot	hottest	hotter		
wet	wettest	wetter		

Suffix Magic Chart O-1

Base Word	Suffix est	Suffix er	Suffix ly	Suffix ful
begin				
stop				
cut				
hot				
wet				

Suffix Magic Chart P

Base Word	Suffix est	Suffix er	Suffix ly	Suffix ful
study		studier		
city				
story				
carry		carrier		
play		player		playful
boy				
buy		buyer		

Suffix Magic Chart P-1

Base Word	Suffix est	Suffix er	Suffix ly	Suffix ful
study				
city				
story				
carry				
play				
boy				
buy				

Compound Word Instruction

Instructor Background

This section will take one week to cover. There will be instructor preparation time needed for making transparencies, the Buddy Partner Practice Sheets, and the Parent/Student Reading Together Coupon.

Compound Word Definition

A compound word is two base words joined together to make one word. Both base words must keep all the letters of each word, such as into and something. Both base words must be complete words on their own such as base and ball, key and board.

Compound Words Lesson One

upon	without	into	maybe
something	sometimes	somewhere	someone
anything	anytime	anywhere	anyone
yourself	myself	whenever	

Compound Words Lesson Two

bedtime	bathtub	baseball	football
downtown	homemade	toothbrush	bookmark
lookout	without	farmyard	backyard
raceway	outside	inside	sailboat
myself			

Compound Words Lesson Three

whichever	housefly	wherever	waterfall
watermelon	watercolor	kindness	handful
backfire	backbone	backing	backpack
sidewalk	lighthouse	lookout	compound

Procedures for Day One

1. Display the first row of the transparency of Compound Words, Lesson One.

2. Tell them they are to figure out what a compound word is. Read the first word, have the students repeat. Continue the same way with the rest of the row.

3. Ask the students what they discovered about these compound words. Help them as needed.

4. Ask the students to name the two words in each compound word. Underline the two words separately.

5. Continue with the second row the same way. Ask what the students noticed alike about the words in the row. (They all use the same first word.)

6. Continue with the third row in the same way. Ask what the students noticed alike about the words in the row. (They all use the same first word.) Ask what the students notice alike about the second and third rows. (Some use the same second word.)

7. Continue with the last row in the same way.

8. Have the students read the words aloud as you point, then read the words as you point to words randomly.

9. Have the students buddy partner practice read.

Procedures for Day Two

1. Display the transparency of Compound Words, Lesson Two.

2. Review what a compound word is.

3. Have the students read through the words silently. Then have them read all rows as you point to the words, first in order, then randomly.

4. Put a number beside each word. Ask the students to choose a word, then to themselves, put it into a sentence.

5. Call on a student to tell his/her sentence. Ask the other students to raise their hands if they know which word was used and tell the word and number. Repeat until all the words have been used.

6. Have the students Buddy Practice read.

Procedures for Day Three

1. Display Compound Words, Lesson Three.

2. Review what a compound word is.

3. Ask the students to read silently through the compound words. Tell them there may be some words on the transparency that are not compound words.

4. Ask the students to read the words in the first row aloud one at a time and say the two words that make it a compound word. As the students tell you, underline the two words that make up each compound word. Help the students know that the word *wherever* is not a compound word because when you underline the two words, you have *where* and *ver*. *Ver* is not a full word.

5. Ask students to read row two to themselves and locate the words that are compound and the ones that are not. Have students read the words aloud while you underline the two words that make up the compound word. They should decide that *kindness* and *handful* are not made up of two words, but are made up of one word and a suffix.

6. Continue in the same manner with row three. All are compound words except *backing*, which is one word with a suffix.

7. Continue in the same manner with row four. All are compound words except *compound*, which is not made up of two complete base words.

8. Have the students Buddy Practice read, circling the words that are not compound.

Procedures for Day Four

1. Provide the students with dictionaries.

2. Ask them to find and write five new compound words. Give them ten to fifteen minutes for this.

3. Gather students together. Have them read their words as you write them on a transparency.

4. Together read all the words, marking the two that make them a compound word, determining if each word is really a compound word.

Procedures for Day Five

1. Staple all Buddy Partner Practice Sheets together, including yesterday's compound words found by the students, and a Parent/Student Homework Reading Together. Have the students write his/her name on the coupon and then allow time for buddy partner practice.

2. When buddy partners finish reading, they put their papers in a specific basket and begin independent silent reading, using the classroom library.

3. *If instructing a group:* Listen to each set of buddy partners read their Buddy Partner Practice Sheets. Select words randomly from the packet for the partners to read. Check the basic understanding and record what needs review later. Write a positive note on each student's Buddy Partner Practice Sheet.

4. Have the partners return to silent reading while you continue to evaluate other students' progress.

5. Students take the Parent/Student Reading Together Coupon packet home to go over with parents and return the following week.

Go to Section 5.

Contraction Instruction

Instructor Background

This section will take one week to cover. There will be instructor preparation time needed for making transparencies, the Buddy Partner Practice Sheets, and the Parent/Student Reading Together Coupon.

A contraction is two words joined together, with one or more letters left out, usually from the second word as in <u>haven't</u>, <u>would've</u>.

Contractions Lesson One

didn't	isn't	wouldn't	couldn't	haven't	aren't
can't	hadn't	don't	shouldn't	wasn't	

Contractions Lesson Two

they'll	you'll	we'll	I'll	he'll	she'll
they'd	you'd	we'd	I'd	he'd	she'd
they've	you've	we've	I've	he's	she's
they're	you're	we're	I'm		

Contractions Lesson Three

it's	where's	let's	won't
would've	should've		

Procedures for Day One

1. Display the first row of the transparency of Contractions, Lesson One.

2. Ask the students to figure out what pattern they see as they read with you. Read the first word, have the students repeat. Continue the same way with the rest of the row.

3. Ask the students what pattern they discovered. Help as needed.

The students should have noticed:

    a. The words all have one complete word at the beginning.

    b. The words all have *n't* after the complete word.

4. Tell the students that these words are called contractions.

5. Have the students tell you the complete word at the beginning, as you underline the first word in the contraction.

6. Ask the students to figure out what the *n't* means. Help as needed. (*N't* stands for the word *not*.)

7. Remind the students these words are called contractions. Ask for the meaning of the word "contract" as you underline the word contract in the word contractions. Explain that contractions are really like compound words, except they have been contracted, or made smaller.

8. Write the sets of words did not, is not, would not, was not, could not. Ask the students to help you to contract the words did and not. Cup your hands around the two words, ask the students to cup their hands around the two words. Pretend you are trying hard to push the words together. Push and push, until finally you say, *Pop!* Quickly make a curved line from the *o* going up and away.

Tell the students they did it! They contracted the word by popping the *o* out and moving the *n* over. Rewrite the words "did not" to say "didn't." Explain that the ' (apostrophe) shows that a letter popped out.

9. Continue in the same manner with the rest of the sets of words from the first row.

10. Ask the students if they think the *n't* will always stand for the word not. *yes.*

11. Continue with the second row the same way. Ask what the students noticed any similarities about the words in the row. They all have a complete word followed by the *n't*, except for the word can't. Explain to them that can't is made up the words can and not. Ask them what letters were popped out. (Letters *n* and *o*

from the second word.) Have the students contract the words in the same manner as in the first row.

12. Have the students buddy partner practice read.

Procedures for Day Two

1. Display the first row of the transparency of Contractions, Lesson Two.

2. Ask the students what a contraction is. Read the first word, have the students repeat. Continue the same way with the rest of the row.

3. Ask the students what pattern they discovered with these contractions. Help as needed. The students should have noticed:

    a. The words all have one complete word at the beginning.

    b. The words all have *'ll* after the complete word.

4. Have the students tell you the complete word at the beginning, as you underline it.

5. Ask the students what the *'ll* means. Help as needed. *'ll* stands for the word will and (') (apostrophe) shows where letters popped out.

6. Write the sets of words they will, you will, we will, I will, he will, she will. Ask the students to help you contract the words they and will. Cup your hands around the two words, ask the students to cup their hands around the two words. Pretend you are trying hard to push the words together. Push and push, until finally you say, *Pop!* Quickly make a curved line going up and away from where the letters *wi* had been.

Tell the students they contracted the word. Ask them what letters popped out. They should notice that two letters popped out, the *wi*. Rewrite the word you and will to make the word you'll. Explain that the ' (apostrophe) shows that one or more letters popped out when the word was contracted to become a contraction.

7. Continue in the same manner with the other word sets written on the transparency.

8. Continue with the second, third, and fourth rows the same way, asking what the students noticed alike about the words in the columns. (They all have the same complete first word.) Have them contract the words in the same manner as in the first row.

Row 2: The *'d* stands for the word *had* or *would*, depending upon meaning of the word in the sentence. The letters *ha* or *woul* "popped" out.

Row 3: The *'ve* stands for the word have, the letters *ha* "popped" out. The *'s* stands for the word is, the letter *i* "popped" out.

Row 4: The *'re* stands for the word are, the letter *a* "popped" out. The *'m* stands for the word am, the letter *a* "popped" out.

9. Have the students buddy partner practice read.

Procedures for Day Three

1. Display the transparency of Contractions, Lesson Three.
2. Ask the students what a contraction is. Read the first word, have the students repeat. Continue the same way with the rest of the row.
3. Ask the students what pattern(s) they discovered about these contractions. Help as needed. The students should have noticed several different things.
4. Continue in the same manner as yesterday. Notice that the word *won't* does not fit the pattern for making contractions. Long ago the words "*will not*" made the contraction *willn't*, but through the years it has changed to *won't*.
5. Have the students buddy partner practice read.

Procedures for Day Four

1. Review what a contraction is.
2. Assign the partners to find a book they have already read from the classroom library. Have them find as many contractions in ten minutes as possible, writing each contraction on paper.
3. Gather students together. Have the students read and spell the words aloud (using the term contraction) as you write them on a transparency.
4. Together, read all the words, naming the two words that make each contraction.

Procedures for Day Five

1. Staple all Buddy Partner Practice Sheets together, including the contractions the students found in books yesterday and a Parent/Student Reading Together Coupon. Have the students write his/her name on the coupon and then allow time for buddy partner practice.

2. When buddy partners finish reading with each other, they put their papers in a specific basket and begin independent silent reading, using the classroom library.

3. *If instructing a group:* Listen to each set of buddy partners read their Buddy Partner Practice Sheets. Listen to the students read all the contractions in the packet. Check the basic understanding and record what needs review later. Write a positive note on each student's Buddy Partner Practice Sheet.

4. Have the partners return to silent reading while you continue to evaluate other students' progress. Students take the Parent/Student Reading Together Coupon packet home to go over with parents and return the following week.

Play the Memory or Puff Game using some contraction words and some suffix words. Go to Unit VI, Section 1.

UNIT VI

HOW TO MAKE SENSE FROM WRITTEN WORDS

Background and Preparation for Teaching Unit VI

Each student must read material useful and meaningful to him/her and be able to understand what he/she is reading. Even though the students are reading material now, it is important to go over each of the following skills.

In Unit VI the students will learn to make reading useful and meaningful by:

1. Using punctuation marks such as periods, question marks, exclamation marks, colons, capitals, commas, and quotation marks.

2. Using the known words in written material to unlock the meaning of individual unknown words.

3. Asking questions to himself/herself while reading and by locating topic sentences in paragraphs.

You and the students are to select books and articles pertinent to the students' current studies, interests, or needs, and at a level the students can comfortably read.

If instructing an individual: You and the student gather materials independently or together. Be sure the materials match the student's interests, needs, and comfort level.

If instructing a group: Gather sets of six to eight books that are alike and pertinent to a current social studies, science, or literature study. Also select several books related to a study that you can use for large group lessons.

If the total group is made up of eighteen students, instruct the students in groups of six. If the total group is made up of twenty-five students, instruct the students in groups of six or seven at a time.

Have each student tell you which two books are especially interesting to him/her. Try to group the students so each one will be reading his/her first or second choice.

Go to Section 2.

Making Reading Sense Using Punctuation

Instructor Background

You will need to know the following punctuation rules:

1. A period (.) is like a stop sign. It tells the reader to stop for a short pause and that a thought has been completed. It is read as if something is being told.

2. A capital letter always begins a sentence.

3. A sentence is a complete thought with a period at the end.

4. A comma (,) tells the reader to make a short pause, a shorter pause than for a period. A thought has not been completed yet.

5. A colon (:) usually tells the reader that a list is coming right after the (:).

6. An exclamation mark (!) tells the reader to read as if surprised.

7. A question mark (?) tells the reader a question is being asked, and the tone of his/her voice goes up at the end of the question.

8. A set of quotation marks (" ") around one or more words, lets the reader know that someone is speaking. The quotation marks are like two hands cupped around what is being said.

9. An *'s* after a name or thing often means something belongs to that name or thing.

Procedures for Day One

1. From a book or article you selected, choose three paragraphs, each with four, five, or six short sentences. Copy each paragraph on its own transparency.

2. Display the transparency with the first paragraph. Ask if the students know what a period is and to come point it out. Ask what the period is telling the reader. "To stop." Have all the periods identified by the students. Ask what always follows a period. "A capitalized word." Ask why. "To tell us another new sentence or complete thought is starting." Ask the students to read the first sentence together aloud. Continue with the next sentences. Encourage them to read as if they're talking.

3. Display the transparency with the second paragraph. Ask how many periods are in the paragraph. Ask, "How many sentences are in the paragraph?" Ask how many capital letters they see. Ask if there were the same number of capital letters as there were periods. Why or why not? Read the sentences together.

4. Display the transparency with the third paragraph. Continue in the same manner as with the first two paragraphs. If there is a capital letter for the name of something, discuss the purpose of that capital.

5. Read in groups from the book sets or with an individual, putting good pauses after periods.

Procedures for Day Two

1. Write a large period, comma, exclamation point, and question mark at the top of a transparency. Under them write sentences, which can use a period, question mark, and an explanation point. For example:

    She is having fun. She is having fun! She is having fun?
    He can run? He can run! He can run.
    Look! Look? Look.

2. On a second transparency, copy two paragraphs from a book readable by the students that use periods, commas, exclamation marks, and question marks.

3. Cover the bottom of the first transparency with paper and display only the . , ! and ?. Ask the students to name the punctuation marks and tell what they tell the reader. Help them as needed.

4. Display the rest of the first transparency. Have the students notice each sentence starts with a capital and ends with a punctuation mark. Count how many commas are in the paragraphs. Read them the way the punctuation marks tell the reader. Have fun!

5. Display the second transparency. First notice the punctuation marks and capitals that are used, then read the sentences with the proper expression.

6. Continue reading in groups or with individuals from the book sets, using correct expressions. Discuss the use of capitals, if used for anything other than the beginning of a sentence.

Procedures for Day Three

1. From a book or article, copy onto a transparency, two paragraphs that use capital letters within a sentence indicating the word is the name of a person, place, or book. Try to choose paragraphs with varied punctuation marks.

2. On a blank transparency, write a sentence that uses a student's name but do not capitalize the name. Ask the students what is wrong with the sentence. Tell them that names of places, things, and people are capitalized.

3. Write another sentence using a student's name, the school's name and the town's name, but do not capitalize any words. Ask them to find the names of people, places, and things. The words to be capitalized are Julie, Booker School, Phoenix, and Outer Space. For example:

> when julie went to booker school in phoenix
> she took her book, outer space.

4. Write the following sentence, but use several students' names in place of the ones now in the sentence: mary, joe, tom and kendra ran to the library so they wouldn't miss the play, "tarzan of the jungle." Library will not be capitalized because it's not the name of the library. Have them notice commas and read the sentence with the correct pauses.

5. Display the transparencies with two paragraphs. Read and notice the use of capitals and punctuation marks.

6. Continue reading in groups or with an individual from the book sets, using correct expressions. Discuss the use of capitals and punctuation marks.

Procedures for Day Four

1. Select materials and copy two paragraphs that use quotation marks.

2. On a blank transparency, write several sentences using quotation marks. For example, "You have learned to read using punctuation marks!" said mother.

3. Ask the students to read the first example. Point out the quotation marks, explain what they mean and how much they look like hands holding together what mother said. Cup your left hand over the first quotation mark and your right hand over the second quotation mark. Have the students do the same thing. Tell them that quotation marks come in twos, just like our hands.

4. Display the transparency with the paragraphs using quotation marks. Have the students read the paragraphs aloud together. Ask if anybody is talking in the paragraphs. Ask them to be "actors" and read only the parts that the characters are saying.

5. Continue reading from the book sets, using correct expressions. Discuss the use of capitals and punctuation marks.

Procedures for Day Five

1. Display a review transparency with punctuation marks and explanations.

2. Review the information with the students.

3. Provide a copy of the transparency for the Buddy Partner Practice Sheet. Add a directive to the parents to listen to the student read the provided book, encouraging the student to read as directed by the punctuation marks. To it, staple a Parent/Student Reading Together Coupon. Have the students write his/her name on the coupon and then allow a brief time for buddy partner practice.

4. Have students select a book to read. Buddy partners should read to each other, practicing good expression as indicated by punctuation marks.

5. *If instructing a group:* Listen to each set of buddy partners read from their chosen book, observing how punctuation marks are used. Write a positive note on each student's Buddy Partner Practice Sheet.

   If instructing an individual: You are the partner, helping and evaluating at the same time. Write a positive note on the Buddy Partner Practice Sheet.

6. Students take the Parent/Student Reading Together Coupon Sheet and book home to read with parents and return the following week.

Go to Section 3.

Understanding Word Meaning Using Context

Instructor Background

When a good reader doesn't recognize a printed word or doesn't know what it means, he/she reads the rest of the sentence to help him/her figure it out. That is called context reading. The reader uses the meaning of other words in the sentence, or sentences around it.

Procedures for Day One

1. On a transparency write ten simple sentences with one blank space where a word should be. Leave space for you to write the word in later. Try to make the sentences relate to something being studied or of interest. For example:

    The worker carried a _(shovel)_ to dig a hole.

    The batter heard the (umpire) shout, "You're out."

2. Display the transparency. Ask the students to read sentence number one aloud together. Ask them what word might fit in the blank and make good sense. There may be several words suggested. Ask what they read in the sentence that made them think their word was right?

3. Write the first two and last two letters of the correct word in the blank. Ask them if that helps them know what the word is. Finish writing the full word and have them read the complete sentence.

4. Continue in the same manner with the other nine sentences. Suggest that when they are reading, they use this technique if there is a word they can't figure out.

a. Read the sentence or paragraph skipping the word(s).

b. Think what words make sense in the sentence(s).

c. Use the first and ending letters to choose the right word(s).

d. Reread the sentence using the word(s) and continue reading.

e. Continue reading in groups from the book sets, using correct expressions. Encourage them to use phonics and the technique outlined above to figure out unknown words.

Procedures for Day Two

1. Copy a paragraph from a book or article that is of particular interest. Leave some words out. In the example below, put in only a blank where the word is underlined:

> As the bright yellow <u>plane</u> rolled to a bumpy stop, the <u>passenger</u> door opened. Out <u>climbed</u> Joe Smith. Tall and <u>slim</u>, he stood at the bottom of the <u>snowy</u> mountain. He planned to make an <u>ascent</u> to the mountain top with three <u>friends.</u>

2. Read the paragraph together. Each time there is a blank, make a short hum for the word. Then use the steps outlined in yesterday's number four lesson.

3. Read a story or book to the students that has some words with meanings unknown to them. Have them use the words and sentences around the unknown words to determine the meaning of the word.

Procedures for Day Three

1. Follow the same plans as on day one but use new sentences.

Procedures for Day Four

1. Follow the same plans as on day two but use a new paragraph. Continue reading the same story or book to the students or read a different one.

Procedures for Day Five

1. Provide copies of the transparencies used during the week for the Buddy Partner Practice Sheets. Include the steps for figuring out new words, listed in day one's number four. Add a directive to the parents to let the students be teacher for them, while the parents try to determine the missing words. To it, staple a Parent/Student Reading Together Coupon. Have the students write their name on the coupon.

2. Review the steps for using context to figure out new words, listed in day one's number four. Tell the students their homework assignment is to teach their parents how to use these steps with the same sentences and paragraphs they used during the week.

3. Give each student a copy of the words that belong in the blanks in the Buddy Partner Practice Sheets. Have the students practice being teacher with their partner.

4. Students take the Parent/Student Reading Together Coupon packet home to do with parents and return the following week.

Go to Section 4.

Understanding What Is Being Read Using Comprehension Skills

This section will take three weeks to complete.

Week One

1. Find or write a very short article or true story of lively interest or use the sample story below. Children's magazines and books are often good sources for articles. Read the story to yourself to find where leading questions might be asked. See questions in the sample story below.

2. Write the title and the story on transparencies, leaving extra space between the sentences where leading questions will be asked.

3. The sample below is an embellished true story and should be broken into three days' lessons, depending on the age and attention span of the students.

Preparation for Day One

1. Explain that a good reader understands what he/she is reading. To do that readers collect knowledge and ask themselves questions as they read. Tell the students that this week's lessons will help them further develop those comprehension skills.

2. Display the first overhead transparency but do not turn on the projector's light.

3. With a sheet of paper, cover all the transparency except the title. Turn on the projector light. Have the students read the story title.

4. If using the sample, ask the suggested questions provided, or some of your own. A younger student will respond with different answers and questions than will an older student. Both may be correct and OK.

5. Move the paper just below number 1, the first sentence, and ask what the students know now. Also ask what they now want to know.

6. Continue with numbers 2, 3, 4, and 5 in the same manner, asking what new information did they learn and what questions do they want answered as they read on. Guide them to think deeper.

Sample Story Title: *The Living Pipe Cleaner*

Suggested instructor questions: What does this tell you about the story? What do you want to find out as you read the story?

Possible student responses: What is the living pipe cleaner? I know what a pipe cleaner looks like but what color and shape is it? How can it be living?

1. The city engineers couldn't figure out how to solve the problem.

Suggested instructor questions: What do you know now? Now what do you want to find out?

Possible student responses: We know the pipe belonged to the city. What kind of pipe was it? How do they clean the pipe? What was the problem? Will they get someone else to help them?

2. The drainage pipes were old and dirty. It took a long time for water to drain through them.

Suggested instructor questions: Did you find the answers to any of your questions? What do you want to find out as you read more?

Possible student responses: We know they were drainage pipes. They drain water. What kind? Storm drains? Above or below ground? Vertical or horizontal? Made of what materials? Something living must help them clean the drainage pipes.

3. When it rained, the city streets often flooded because the pipes couldn't drain much water at a time. Those dirty old drainage pipes caused other problems, too.

Suggested instructor questions: Same as for 2.

Possible student responses: We know the pipes were old; they caused water to back up and flood. The pipes drain rain water. Still want to know how they clean the pipes. What were the other problems? Maybe mud slides.

4. Cars stalled. Buildings got water in them. The city's citizens didn't want to go shopping. Parents wouldn't send their children to school.

Suggested instructor questions: Same as for 2.

Possible student responses: They had lots of problems. Did the schools and stores have to close? What did it cost the city to cope with these problems?

5. The engineers tried to use their big, expensive equipment to clean the pipes, but the equipment wouldn't fit in the pipes. They called the plumber to try his rotary drill, but it wasn't long enough.

Suggested instructor questions: Did you find answers to any of your questions? What do you know about their equipment? What did they do? Why? What do you want to find out?

Possible student responses: Know they tried to solve the problem themselves and with outside help. Knew they didn't get the problem fixed. How do they fix the pipes? Were the citizens getting mad?

Preparation for Day Two

1. On the lit overhead display the transparencies with the title, *The Living Pipe Cleaner,* and the words of the story contained in numbers 1 through 5, above.

2. Read aloud with the students.

3. Review what they wanted to find out as they continued the story.

4. Place the transparency containing number 6 on the unlit overhead projector.

5. Tell them as they read more of the story, they will be developing comprehension skills by thinking what they learned new, and what else they want to know.

6. Cover the transparency with a plain paper so only number 6 shows. Turn on the projector light.

7. Continue in the same manner with numbers 6 through 12 using the same process that was used yesterday.

Continuation of Sample Story, *The Living Pipe Cleaner*

6. The dirty pipes were two blocks long, much too long. What could they use? How could they clean the pipes? They asked for ideas from the citizens.

Possible student responses: Know they asked citizens for help. Maybe there were experts among them. What ideas did the citizens have? Know how long the pipes were.

7. The second grade class at Elbert School thought their pet ferret might help.

Possible student responses: The children wanted to help. How could a little ferret help? A ferret couldn't be big enough for the pipe. They still need outside expert help.

8. They had noticed their furry pet liked to get in dark places and go exploring. The class wanted to volunteer their ferret to crawl through the pipe, but they didn't want to lose him. They had a problem-solving session.

Possible student responses: Is the ferret the living pipe cleaner? It's too small. Engineers shouldn't accept the class' idea, they should tell the class that the pipe is too big. The class must like to solve problems. Ferrets are furry, like dark places and exploring. The class really likes the ferret.

9. The class decided to tie a strong twine onto their ferret's collar and one-half of the class would quietly put him in the pipe's entrance. The other half of the class would go to the pipe's exit with the ferret's favorite food and call to the ferret. The city engineers would have to help with the rest of the plan.

Possible student responses: The class found a solution. What's the rest of the plan? Know the ferret will pull a twine through, but why? How long was the twine? Ferret is still not big enough to do any good.

10. One city engineer told the class it just *couldn't* work, but the rest of the city engineers liked the class' idea. They busily prepared to help the second grade class. The next day a big crowd gathered to see how the plan would work.

Possible student responses: Just one engineer thought their idea was not good. The city was very interested in seeing the plan in action. What was the class' idea? What did the city have to prepare? Does it work? Are they still going to use the ferret? It's too small. They need an expert's help.

11. Just as planned, the ferret slipped right into the entrance of the long, dark pipe. The second graders at the exit called to their pet. The little ferret scooted along the two-block-long pipe toward the second graders, exploring all the way to the exit.

Possible student responses: Will the ferret go all the way through the pipe? Will the twine still be attached to the ferret? How long was the twine? As long as the two-block-long pipe? What did the engineers prepare to do? How did this solve the problem?

12. Out the ferret popped, dragging the twine behind it. The little ferret wasn't even dirty! While it gobbled its favorite food, the workers detached the twine.

Possible student responses: The plan worked. The twine was still attached, but how long was it? Why did they do it? The ferret wasn't dirty! Why? Maybe the pipe wasn't dirty and doesn't need to be cleaned out. Maybe the ferret was so small its fur didn't rub against the debris in the pipe. What will the workers do with the twine? It must have been the full length of the pipe.

Procedures for Day Three

1. On the lit overhead display the transparencies with the title, *The Living Pipe Cleaner,* and the story contained in numbers 1 through 12.

2. Read aloud with the students.

3. Review what they wanted to find out as they continued the last part of the story.

4. Place the transparency containing number 13 on the unlit overhead projector.

5. Tell them as they read more of the story, they will be developing comprehension skills by thinking what they learned new and what else they want to know.

6. Cover the transparency with plain paper so only number 13 shows. Turn on the projector light.

7. Continue in the same manner with numbers 13 through 19 using the same process that was used yesterday.

Continuation of Sample Story, *The Living Pipe Cleaner*

13. The workers at the pipe's exit informed the workers at the pipe's entrance that the ferret made it through the pipe with the twine still attached. Workers at the entrance attached a very long strong rope onto the strong twine. The workers at the exit pulled the twine through the pipe until they got the strong rope. They informed the workers at the entrance that they had the rope. The workers at the entrance now attached a cable onto the strong rope.

Possible student responses: The twine was as long as the pipe. The little ferret did help. How did the workers talk to each other? With walkie talkies? The workers put a stronger material on the twine, then on the rope. What will they attach next?

14. With a machine, the workers at the exit pulled the stronger rope with the cable behind it, all the way to the pipe's exit. With their new telephones, they informed the workers at the entrance that they had the cable. The workers at the entrance attached a huge stiff round wire brush, a little larger than the pipe's diameter.

Possible student responses: The cable must be hard to pull through. It took a machine to pull it. There is resistance when they pull the cable. They used a new telephone to communicate. The brush is bigger than the pipe. It will be hard to pull. What will they use to pull the brush through the pipe? The same machine, bigger machine, horses? Something pretty strong. Will it clean the pipe or was that the problem?

15. At the pipe's exit, three husky workers were connecting the end of the cable to the front of a strange looking machine. The machine roared as it started. Its operator slowly backed up, backing up as the machine pulled and tried to turn the cable round and round. Suddenly the machine lurched, sputtered, and came to a dead stop. The operator couldn't get it started again.

Possible student responses: The cable was heavy. They used a different machine, but it quit on them. What kind of a machine did they use? How did they get this new problem solved?

16. The city engineers got their heads together to figure out what to do. The workers got their heads together to figure out what to do. The second graders got their heads together to figure out what to do. They even asked Tommy's dad to join them for awhile. Then the city engineers, the workers, the second graders, and Tommy's dad <u>all</u> got their heads together. They decided to try a different machine.

Possible student responses: Each group of people must have brainstormed before they got together to share their solutions. They agreed to try a different machine. What was the different machine? Will it work?

17. The cable was attached to the back of the Tommy's dad's big farm tractor. It roared to life with a forward jerk. Slowly the tractor moved down one block and down the second block, pulling behind it the large rotating cable.

Possible Student Responses: The new machine was a farm tractor. The cable was turning round and round. How? The tractor must have had a take-off drive. The cable with the brush was being pulled through the two-block-long pipe. Will it clean anything out of the pipe? How did the citizens feel?

18. The watching crowd saw a huge growing pile of leaves, twigs, rusty scales, and dirt forming on the ground outside the pipe's exit until finally the big round wire brush came out. The plan had worked. The turning brush had pushed debris out of the pipe as the tractor pulled it forward.

Possible student responses: The pipe was dirty. What did they give the students as a reward? The farmer? The ferret? The workers?

19. Tommy's dad heard the citizens cheer from two blocks away. The next day the mayor gave the second grade class a "Great Problem Solvers'" plaque and each student a big blue ribbon. He gave the ferret a year's supply of its favorite food and a pipe to explore. The words, "The Living Pipe Cleaner," were engraved on the pipe.

Possible student responses: The citizens were really happy. Tommy's dad heard the cheer from two blocks away. The problem was solved. Just the second grade class and the ferret got awards. Still want to know what the ferret's favorite food was. Now we know how the story got it's name.

Possible teacher's response: Now we have a problem to solve. How could we find out what a ferret's favorite food might be? Let's do it.

Preparation for Day Four

1. Find out what a ferret's favorite food is, using the students suggestions for getting the information.
2. Provide a copy of the story *The Living Pipe Cleaner* for each student to read silently. Ask the students what places in the story should have an illustration. Share the decisions.
3. Tell the students that illustrations include what was learned from the text and often contain additional information.
4. Assign the illustrations to be made by the students. Ask them to use information learned from the text but also to include some additional information in their illustration.
5. Collect the story copies.

Preparation for Day Five

1. Paste together a large book using the story text and the student illustrations.

2. Explain to the students that part of comprehension is studying the illustrations, graphs, or tables included with the text.

3. Read the book together, looking carefully at each illustration. Discuss each illustration, finding what information the artist included that was included in the text. Also search each illustration for new information that wasn't included in the text.

4. Provide copies of the story *The Living Pipe Cleaner.* Include an explanation of the comprehension skills worked on during the week. Add a directive to the parents to let the students be teacher for them. They will have the parents read just a part of the story, then ask them what they learned and what they want to know. Staple to it a Parent/Student Reading Together Coupon. Have the student write his/her name on the coupon.

5. Tell the students their homework assignment is to teach their parents how to use the comprehension skills that they learned. They will have the parent read part of the story, then ask them what they learned and what they want to know.

6. Students take the Parent/Student Reading Together Coupon packet home to do with parents and return the following week.

Week Two

Using a story or article of your choice, repeat the first week's procedures. The students will not need as much guidance this time. They will have more fun with it. If you have time, repeat the procedure with another story or article. Send them home on Friday along with the Student/Parent Reading Together Coupon for the students to be the teacher again with their parents.

Week Three
Procedures

1. Select a nonfiction book that contains well written paragraphs and is relative to the students' current interest. If instructing a group, obtain as many copies of the book as possible.

2. Copy onto transparencies, the title and all the paragraphs from story below, *Siberian Tigers in Trouble*.

3. Copy onto transparencies five or six paragraphs from the non-fiction book you selected. Write a title for the paragraphs.

4. Copy onto transparencies *only* the topic sentences from five or six additional paragraphs from the nonfiction book you selected and a title for them.

Siberian Tigers in Trouble

The Siberian tiger is an endangered species, mostly because of poaching. Poachers hunt for Siberian tigers to earn money. They can earn as much as twenty thousand dollars for each dead tiger. Some of the tiger's body parts are used to make medicine. The skins of the Siberian tiger are trophies to some of Russia's rich people.

Because of a diminishing habitat, there are also fewer Siberian tigers. Once there were thousands of Siberian tigers roaming the forests of Eastern Russia, and of far northern China and Korea. Now there are fewer than five hundred Siberian tigers still living wild in the cold, lonely, snowy Russian Far East.

The Siberian tiger is one of nature's most magnificent creatures. Beautifully marked with uneven, symmetrical black stripes on orange, they also have white jowls and undersides. Golden eyes glow below a broad striped forehead. When a Siberian tiger roars, its lips draw back to show the huge, sharply-pointed-canine teeth. Weighing as much as 800 pounds, the tiger's huge paws easily walk over the snow.

An effort is being made to save the Siberian tigers from extinction. A group called the Siberian Tiger Project has radio-collared nine Siberian tigers and is now studying them in the wild to determine their range. They have also rescued cubs of tigers who were killed.

Zoos have been receiving some Siberian tigers that were rescued. Sometimes it is necessary to capture the cubs to save their lives. When that happens, the captive cubs can't be released back to the wild. They are firmly imprinted on humans after they're one year old. Even though the Siberian tiger cubs still have the wild tiger spirit, they must go to a zoo in order to survive.

One member of the Siberian Tiger Project says that the best hope for the Siberian tigers survival in the wild, is to protect them and their habitat. But if disaster should strike, the zoo-bred tigers will allow the species to live.

Procedures for Day One

1. Explain that this week they will be learning how to read non-fiction books for the best understanding by using topic sentences.

2. Display the transparency with the title and paragraph one.

3. Cover everything except the title. Ask what they might expect to be learning.

4. Uncover only the first paragraph. Explain that a paragraph usually gives information about one part of the article or book. Explain that a paragraph can be identified because it is indented from the margin. The rest of the paragraph text goes out to the margin.

5. Read the first sentence together. Tell the students that usually the first sentence in a paragraph tells what the paragraph will be about. The rest of the paragraph gives details about the first sentence. This is especially true in nonfiction (true) books. That sentence is called a topic sentence. Ask what this paragraph will be about. Underline the topic sentence with a marker.

6. Have the students read the rest of the paragraph to learn the details about Siberian tigers being poached.

7. Cover all the paragraph except the topic sentence. Ask what details were given about poaching, which is endangering the Siberian tiger.

8. Display only the topic sentence in paragraph two. Read together. Ask what they expect to learn. Underline the topic sentence with a marker.

9. Display the rest of the paragraph and ask for it to be read silently.

10. Cover all the paragraph except the topic sentence. Ask what details were given about the Siberian tigers' habitat getting smaller. Be prepared to use a map to show the area under discussion.

11. Display the topic sentence in paragraph three. Follow steps in numbers eight, nine, and ten.

12. Ask students to identify the indentations and topic sentences in each paragraph.

13. Ask them to read along with you only the title and the topic sentences. Explain that by reading just that much, they know what informational details will be included in the rest of the text.

Procedures for Day Two

1. Review the meaning of indentation, paragraphs, topic sentences, and details.

2. Display paragraph four. Have the students identify the topic sentence. Underline it with a marker.

3. Ask what the details in the paragraph will be about. Have them read the paragraph to themselves. Cover the topic sentence and discuss the details.

4. Continue in the same manner with paragraphs five and six.

5. Read the article title and all topic sentences. Ask if they know what the main information is in the article.

6. If the students were looking for information about Siberian tigers in zoos, which paragraph would they read. If that was the only information they were looking for, would it be necessary to read the details in every paragraph?

Procedures for Day Three

1. Display the overhead transparency of the title and five or six factual paragraphs from the nonfiction book.

2. Read through it together, using the same procedures that were used for *Siberian Tigers in Trouble.*

3. Ask in which paragraphs the students would find certain specific information. (As was done the previous day in number six.)

Procedures for Day Four

1. Display the final set of five or six additional paragraph title and topic sentences.

2. Together read the title and all the topic sentences from the paragraphs. Observe that they told you all the main thoughts of what the article was about.

3. Ask in which paragraphs the students would find certain specific information.

4. Provide the students with the book from which the topic sentences were copied. Ask them to locate and read the details that went with each paragraph. If you are instructing a group, you may want to have the students work with a buddy partner or in a small group under your supervision.

5. Call the students together to read the title and then the first topic sentence.

6. Ask the students to tell what details they found to go with the first topic sentence.

7. Repeat number six with the other topic sentences.

Procedures for Day Five

1. Read together for twenty minutes from the factual book that was used for day three and four's lessons. If instructing a group, form smaller groups and meet with each group, so you can guide them.

2. As you read the first page:

   a. Ask how many paragraphs are on the page.

   b. Read the page's topic sentences first.

   c. Read the full page.

   d. Ask in which paragraph specific details (named by you) are located; for instance, which paragraph describes the cave's interior.

3. On the next page:

   a. Ask how many paragraphs are on the page.

   b. Read the full page.

    c. Ask in which paragraph specific details (named by you) are located.

    d. Ask how they knew so quickly.

4. Copy and staple together the week's lessons used on the overhead projector and also the Parent/Student Reading Together Coupon. Explain to the students that they will be teachers, giving the lessons to their parents.

Congratulations! Celebrate! You have given the gift of lifetime reading to your students. You and your students have completed the steps in *You Can Teach Someone to Read*. Encourage them to continue independent reading. Perhaps you'll want to give a congratulations gift—a book you know will be read and loved with pleasant memories.

APPENDIXES

Consonant Sounds

All the alphabet letters except the vowels *Aa, Ee, Ii, Oo,* and *Uu* are consonants. When the name of the consonant letter is said, some part of the mouth has to touch another part of the mouth for the letter to be a consonant. Of the 21 consonant letters, 13 of them have single sounds. The other eight consonants have more than one sound. *Yy* and *Ww* are a consonant and vowel but are a consonant most of the time. Knowing the sounds of the consonants helps the reader to figure out unknown words.

The Thirteen Consonants With Single Sounds

Bb as in <u>b</u>oy   *Dd* as in <u>d</u>og   *Ff* as in <u>f</u>un   *Hh* as in <u>h</u>ello
Jj as in <u>j</u>ello   *Kk* as in <u>k</u>itten   *Ll* as in <u>l</u>ion   *Mm* as in <u>m</u>an
Pp as in <u>p</u>et   *Rr* as in <u>r</u>un   *Tt* as in <u>t</u>oy   *Vv* as in <u>v</u>iolet
Zz as in <u>z</u>oo

The Eight Consonants With More Than One Sound

Cc as in <u>c</u>ity   The consonant *Cc* immediately followed by an *e, i,* or *y,* usually has its soft *Ss* sound as in <u>c</u>enter and <u>c</u>ycle.

Cc as in <u>c</u>ake   The consonant *Cc* <u>not</u> immediately followed by an *e, i,* or *y,* usually has the sound of *Kk* as in <u>c</u>at and cy<u>c</u>le.

Gg as in <u>g</u>em   The consonant *Gg* immediately followed by an *e, i,* or *y,* often has the sound of *Jj* as in <u>g</u>iraffe and <u>g</u>ypsy.

Gg as in <u>g</u>oat	The consonant *Gg* <u>not</u> immediately followed by an *e, i,* or *y,* often has its own hard sound as in <u>g</u>ate and <u>g</u>rass.
Nn as in <u>n</u>ose	The consonant *Nn* usually has its own sound as in <u>n</u>o and <u>n</u>est.
n as in sa<u>ng</u>	The consonant *n* immediately followed by *g,* often sounds like *n* and *g* are beginning to swallow their sounds as in si<u>ng</u> and sti<u>ng</u>.
n as in si<u>nk</u>	The consonant *n* immediately followed by *k,* usually sounds like *n* is beginning to swallow its sound, while *k* has its own sound as in ta<u>nk</u> and ri<u>nk</u>.
Qq as in <u>q</u>uick	The consonant *Qq* has <u>no</u> sound of its own. *Qq* must have the vowel *u* immediately after it. Then *qu* has the sound of *k* and *w* together as in <u>q</u>uiet and <u>q</u>uill.
Ss as in <u>s</u>at	The consonant *Ss* usually has its own soft sound as in <u>s</u>oft and <u>s</u>oup.
Ss as in <u>s</u>ure	The consonant *Ss* immediately followed by the letter *u,* sometimes has the sound of *sh* as in <u>s</u>ure and <u>s</u>ugar.
s as in no<u>se</u>	The consonant *s* at the end of a word, immediately followed by an *e,* has the sound of *z* as in clo<u>se</u> and ro<u>se</u>.
Ww as in <u>w</u>et	*Ww* is a consonant when it's at the beginning of a word. Then it usually has its own sound as in <u>w</u>in and <u>w</u>ish.
w as in sa<u>w</u>	*w* is a vowel when it immediately follows the vowels *a, e,* or *o.* Then the *w* combines with the vowel *a, e,* or *o* and has a new vowel sound as in s<u>aw</u>, n<u>ew</u>, h<u>ow</u>, and sn<u>ow</u>.
x as in bo<u>x</u>	The consonant *x* at the inside or end of a word, usually has the sound of the letters *k* and *s* together as in si<u>x</u> and a<u>x</u>le.

Xx as in xylophone The consonant *X* at the beginning of a word has the sound of *z* as in xenon and xylophone.

Yy as in yes   *Yy* is always a consonant when it's at the beginning of a word and usually has its own sound as in yellow and yet.

y as in play   *y* is a vowel when the letters *ay* are together. Then *ay* has the long sound of *a* as in say and may.

y as in cry   *y* is a vowel when it's at the end of a short one syllable word. Then *y* usually has the long *i* vowel sound as in my and fry.

y as in puppy   *y* is a vowel when it's at the end of a longer word with two or more syllables. Then *y* usually has the long *e* vowel sound as in baby and funny.

Two Consonants Together with One Sound

Sometimes when two consonant letters are together, they have one unvoiced sound, such as *sh, ch, ck,* and *ph.*

The consonants *ch* can be anywhere in a word and usually have the sound as in church and each.

The consonants *sh* can be anywhere in a word and usually have the sound as in shop and fish.

The consonants *ck* usually follows a single vowel which has a short sound and is in the middle or end of words. *Ck* usually has the sound of *k* as in back and pocket.

The consonants *ph* can be anywhere in a word and usually have the sound of *f* as in telephone and phrase.

———————————

The two consonant letters *th* and *wh* may have an unvoiced <u>and</u> voiced sound.

The consonants *th* may have an unvoiced or voiced sound when they are at the beginning or the middle or the end of a word as in thought and mother.

The consonants *th* usually have an unvoiced sound when they are at the end of a word as in with.

The letters *wh* usually have an unvoiced sound and are usually at the beginning of a word as in <u>wh</u>ale, <u>wh</u>ip, <u>wh</u>eel, <u>wh</u>ite.

The letters *wh* may have a voiced sound as in <u>wh</u>o.

Vowel Sounds

The vowels are *Aa, Ee, Ii, Oo, and Uu*. When the name of the vowel letter is said, no part of the mouth has to touch another part of the mouth for the letter to be a vowel. *Aa, Ee, Ii, Oo,* and *Uu* each have a long and short vowel sound. Some of the time *Yy* and *Ww* are vowels. Knowing the vowel sounds helps the reader figure out unknown words.

Long Vowel Sounds

The long vowel sound of each vowel sounds like its name.

Aa	as in ape and hay
Ee	as in see and leap
Ii	as in like and child
Oo	as in hope and soap
Uu	as in use and blue

Short Vowel Sounds

The short vowel sounds each have a new sound.

Aa	as in flat and apple
Ee	as in met and egg
Ii	as in sit and igloo
Oo	as in lot and octopus
Uu	as in cup and umbrella

W and Y (See Appendix G, Phonics Rules)

W is only a vowel when it is with another vowel.

Y is a vowel only in the middle or the end of a word. Then it may have the sound of long or short *I* or long *E*.

Sight Words
Unit II, Sections 4 - 14

Each of these sight words should be recalled within five seconds by the completion of Unit II, Section 14.

a	I	other	they
about	in	out	to
and	into	over	was
are	is	part	water
been	it	people	were
come	long	said	what
could	look	see	which
do	many	some	who
each	number	that	word
find	of	the	would
from	oil	their	you
have	one	there	your

Phonetic Words

Unit II, Sections 4 through 14 and Unit III, Sections 2 through 8

Words that can be sounded out using phonics and should be well known at the completion of Unit III, Section 9.

add	can	gave	hurt	me	place
all	close	get	if	men	plant
also	cry	girl	its	mile	play
always	cut	go	just	miss	quack
an	day	got	land	more	quick
as	did	had	last	much	quit
ask	down	hand	late	my	rose
at	end	has	left	name	run
away	face	he	let	next	same
back	fall	help	life	nice	say
be	fast	her	like	no	set
best	first	here	line	now	she
beg	fish	him	list	off	side
but	five	his	made	on	sit
by	fly	home	make	or	six
call	for	hot	man	page	small
came	form	how	may	pick	so

spell	take	these	up	well	why
state	talk	this	us	went	will
stick	tell	those	use	when	wish
story	ten	time	walk	while	with
still	than	try	was	white	write
stop	them	turn	way	who	
such	then				

Sight and Phonetic Words
Unit II, Sections 4 through 14 and Unit III, Sections 2 through 8

These words should be well learned by the end of Unit III.

a	by	first	he	land	mile
about	call	fish	help	last	miss
add	came	five	her	late	more
all	can	fly	here	left	much
also	close	for	him	let	my
always	come	form	his	life	name
an	could	from	home	like	next
and	cry	gave	hot	line	nice
are	cut	get	how	list	no
as	day	girl	hurt	long	not
ask	did	go	I	look	now
at	do	goes	if	made	number
away	down	going	in	make	of
back	each	got	into	man	off
be	end	had	is	many	oil
been	fall	hand	it	may	on
big	fast	has	its	me	one
but	find	have	just	men	or

other	run	state	them	us	which
out	same	stick	then	use	while
over	said	still	there	walk	white
page	say	stop	these	was	who
part	see	story	they	water	why
people	set	such	this	wax	will
pick	she	talk	those	way	wish
place	side	take	time	we	with
plant	sit	tell	to	sell	word
play	six	ten	try	sent	would
quack	small	than	turn	were	write
quick	so	that	two	what	you
quit	some	the	up	when	your
rose	spell	their			

Sight and Phonetic Word

Unit IV, Sections 1 through 10

Words to be well learned by the completion of Unit IV.

above	better	coast	every	gnaw
after	between	coat	example	goat
again	board	cold	eye	goes
air	boat	color	family	going
almost	body	cook	far	good
along	book	country	farther	great
America	both	cow	father	green
animal	boy	different	feet	group
another	bring	does	few	grow
answer	buy	done	fold	hand
any	car	don't	follow	hard
around	carry	draw	food	head
awful	change	drink	found	high
baby	child	earth	four	hoard
because	children	eat	friend	hold
before	city	eight	full	home
begin	clean	enough	funny	house
below	coal	even	give	idea

important	mother	put	sign	toy
Indian	mountain	queen	sing	tree
ink	move	quiet	sleep	under
keep	music	read	snow	until
kind	myself	real	soap	upon
knee	near	right	soar	very
know	need	ring	sold	voice
large	never	river	something	walk
laugh	new	road	sometimes	want
law	night	roar	song	war
learn	noise	roast	soon	warm
leave	often	round	sound	wash
letter	old	rung	start	watch
light	once	saw	study	where
little	only	school	taught	wild
live	open	sea	thank	without
loathe	our	second	think	work
lock	own	seem	thought	world
long	paper	sentence	three	wrap
low	part	seven	through	wrong
mean	phone	shall	toast	year
might	photo	shook	today	yellow
moat	picture	should	together	young
mold	point	show	too	zoo
most	pull	sight	took	

Rules Used to Figure Out Words

These are numbered in the order they are in the book, based on their importance.

RULE 1. If there is only one vowel in a short word with consonants on both sides of it, the vowel usually has its short sound as in the words s<u>a</u>ck and p<u>a</u>l.

RULE 2. If there is only one vowel in a short word, and it's at the end of the word, the vowel usually has its long sound as in the words m<u>e</u> and cr<u>y</u>.

RULE 3. In a short word, if there is only one consonant between a single vowel and an *E* at the end of a word, the single vowel usually has its long sound and the *E* at the end is silent as in the words m<u>ule</u> and s<u>ale</u>.

To mark the silent *E* and long vowel sound, draw a vertical line through the *E* and hop the line over the consonant to make the symbol for a long vowel sound, a straight line over the vowel.

RULE 4. If the only vowel in a very short word is at the beginning of the word, that vowel usually has its short sound as in the words <u>a</u>sh and <u>i</u>tch.

RULE 5. The two vowels *AY* or *AI* together in a word usually have the long *A* sound, while the *Y* or *I* is silent as in st<u>ay</u> and r<u>ai</u>n.

RULE 6. The two vowels *OW* often have the sound of *OW!* as in h<u>ow</u> and d<u>ow</u>n. Sometimes *OU* also has the sound of *OW!* as in h<u>ou</u>se. (More about *OU* sound in Rule 25.)

RULE 7. The two letters *OR* together often have the sound of the word <u>or</u> as in f<u>or</u> and st<u>or</u>y.

RULE 8. The two letters *IR, ER,* and *UR* usually have the sound as in the words h<u>er</u>, sh<u>ir</u>t and f<u>ur</u>.

RULE 9. When the letters *AL* are together, the *A* usually has the sound as in <u>al</u>l. Sometimes the *L* makes its sound as in sm<u>all</u> and h<u>al</u>t. Sometimes the *L* is silent when followed by a *K* as in w<u>alk</u> and t<u>alk</u>.

Rule 10 - 18 are suffix rules.

A suffix is an ending added onto a base word.

RULE 10. Most of the time, just add the suffix if a short base word ends with two consonants, two vowels or two vowels before a single consonant as in walk<u>ed</u>, show<u>s</u> and load<u>ing</u>.

RULE 11. Suffix *S* has the *sound* of the letter *S* as in number<u>s</u> and play<u>s</u>. It is not a syllable.

RULE 12. The suffix *ES* may be added to a base word that ends with the voiceless sound of *O, S, SH, CH,* or *J* as in bush<u>es</u> and wish<u>es</u>. The *ES* sounds like the letter *S'* name, except when it follows *O*. Then *ES* often has the <u>sound</u> of the letter *S*. Suffix *ES* is usually a syllable.

RULE 13. Suffix *ED* is added to a base word that ends with a vowel or voiced consonant sound. The suffix *ED* then has the *D* sound as in play<u>ed</u>, fill<u>ed</u>, and lean<u>ed</u>. This is the way the suffix *ED* is used most of the time. It is not a syllable.

RULE 14. Suffix *ED* is added to a base word that ends with a voiceless consonant sound. The suffix ed then has the *T* sound as in help<u>ed</u>, look<u>ed</u>, and wish<u>ed</u>. This is the way the suffix *ED* is used some of the time. It is not a syllable.

RULE 15. Suffix *ED* is added to a base word that ends with the *D* or *T* sound. The suffix *ED* then sounds like the boy's name, Ed as in want<u>ed</u>, shout<u>ed</u> and load<u>ed</u>. This is the way the suffix *ED* is used the least. It is a syllable.

RULE 16. Suffix *ING* has the sound as in start<u>ing</u> and bark<u>ing</u>. Suffix *ING* is a syllable.

RULE 17. Silent *E* is removed, dropped, from the end of a base word if a suffix with a vowel at the beginning is added as in lin<u>ed</u> and fil<u>ing</u>. Now there is only one consonant between the vowel in the middle of the base word and the vowel at the beginning of a suffix. This usually indicates there *had been* a silent *E* at the end of the base word, and the vowel in the middle will have its long sound.

RULE 18. Silent *E* sometimes has two jobs at the end of a base word. It may indicate the vowel in the middle has a long vowel sound and that *C* or *G* has a soft sound as in pag<u>ed</u> and fac<u>es</u>.

RULE 19. The consonant *C* immediately followed by an *E, I, or Y*, usually has its soft *S* sound as in <u>c</u>enter and <u>c</u>ycle.

RULE 20. The consonant *C not* immediately followed by an *E, I,* or *Y*, usually has the sound of *K* as in <u>c</u>at and cy<u>c</u>le.

RULE 21. The consonant *G* immediately followed by an *E, I, or Y*, often has the soft sound of *J* as in <u>g</u>iraffc and <u>g</u>ypsy.

RULE 22. The consonant *G not* immediately followed by an *E, I, or Y*, often has its own hard sound as in <u>g</u>ate and <u>g</u>rass.

RULE 23. Two *E's* together have the sound of long *E*, as in b<u>ee</u> and k<u>ee</u>p.

RULE 24. The vowels *EA* together have more than one sound. They can have:

    1. the long *E* sound *a lot of the time* as in r<u>ea</u>ch and s<u>ea</u>.

    2. the short EE sound some of the time as in h<u>ea</u>d and h<u>ea</u>vy.

    3. the long *A* sound once in awhile as in gr<u>ea</u>t and br<u>ea</u>k.

4. the sound of *ER*, if the *R* is immediately after *EA* as in h<u>ear</u>d and l<u>ear</u>n.

There is no real rule to know when or why *EA* makes these sounds. The reader should first try the long sound of *E*. If that doesn't work, then use the words around it to help figure it out.

RULE 25. The vowels *OO* together have the short *OO* sound as in sh<u>oo</u>k and b<u>oo</u>k or the long *OO* sound as in z<u>oo</u> and p<u>oo</u>l. .

RULE 26. The vowels *OI* at the beginning or in the middle of a word, and the letters *OY*, usually at the end of a word, usually have the sound of *OI* as in the word <u>oi</u>l, n<u>oi</u>se and empl<u>oy</u>. .

RULE 27. The vowels *OU* together have more than one sound. They can have:

    1. *OW!* as in <u>ou</u>t and ab<u>ou</u>t

    2. short *OO* as in c<u>ou</u>ld and w<u>ou</u>ld

    3. long *OO* as in thr<u>ou</u>gh

    4. short *O* as in th<u>ou</u>ght

    5. short *U* as in y<u>ou</u>ng

    6. long *O* as in y<u>our</u>

There is no way to know which sound *OU* will make in a word. The reader has to use the words around it to help figure out what the word says.

RULE 28. The consonant *Nn* immediately followed by *G*, often sounds like *N* and *G* are beginning to swallow their sounds as in si<u>ng</u> and sti<u>ng</u>.

RULE 29. The consonant *N* immediately followed by *K*, usually sounds like *N* is beginning to swallow its sound, while *K* has its own sound as in ta<u>nk</u> and ri<u>nk</u>.

RULE 30. The vowel *I* immediately followed by *LD* or *ND*, when the letters *ILD* or *IND* are at the end of a one-syllable word, usually has the long *I* sound as in w<u>ild</u> and f<u>ind</u>.

RULE 31. The letters *IGH* usually have the long *i* sound as in h<u>igh</u> and l<u>igh</u>t.

RULE 32. The two vowels *OW* at the end of a short word usually have the long *O* sound as in sh<u>ow</u> and thr<u>ow</u>.

RULE 33. The vowel *O* immediately followed by *LD*, when the letters *OLD* are at the end of a short word, usually has the long *O* sound as in h<u>old</u> and b<u>old</u>.

RULE 34. When the vowels OA are together the O will almost always make its long sound, as in road.

RULE 35. The letters *AR* usually sound like the name of the letter *R* as in c<u>ar</u> and m<u>ar</u>ket.

RULE 36. The letters *WAR* usually have the sound as in <u>war</u>t and <u>war</u>m.

RULE 37. The vowels *WA*, if they are the only vowels in the word and not followed by an *R*, often have the sound as in <u>wa</u>nd, <u>wa</u>sp and <u>wa</u>sh.

RULE 38. The letters *WOR* usually have the sound as in <u>wor</u>ship and <u>wor</u>m.

RULE 39. The letters *GN* at the beginning of a word usually have the sound of *N,* and the *G* is silent as in <u>gn</u>aw and <u>gn</u>ome.

RULE 40. The letters *KN* at the beginning of a word usually have the sound of *N,* and the *K* is silent as in <u>kn</u>ow and <u>kn</u>ee.

RULE 41. The letters *WR* at the beginning of a word usually have the sound of *R,* and the *W* is silent as in <u>wr</u>ite and <u>wr</u>ap.

RULE 42. The vowels *AU* and *AW* usually have the short O sound as in p<u>au</u>se and t<u>au</u>ght, p<u>aw</u>, and sh<u>aw</u>l.

RULE 43. If the two consonants together are ch, sh, th, ck, wh, ng, nk, ph, kn, gn, wr, they make just one sound. But when other consonants are together in sets of two or three, their individual sounds will blend or smoosh together. They are bl, cl, pl, fl, gl, sl, br, cr, pr, fr, gr, dr, tr, sc, sk, sm, sn, sp, sw, st, squ, scr, str, spl, spr. They will usually be at beginning or middle of a word. The blends mp, nd, ft, nt, tch and nch will usually be at the end of a word.

Rules 44 - 47 are syllable rules.

A syllable is a *word part* which contains one vowel sound. Each *vowel sound* in a word is called a *vowel unit*.

RULE 44. Each syllable has one vowel sound.

RULE 45. When *Y* is at the end of a longer word of two or more syllables, Y has the sound of long *E*. *Y* becomes a syllable along with the consonants in front of it OR a syllable of its own.

RULE 46. If there are two consonants together between vowel sounds and they don't have to stay together to make one sound, the word usually divides between them.

RULE 47. If there is only one consonant between the vowel units, usually the word divides in front of the consonant. The vowel in the front has its long sound. If the word doesn't sound right, divide the word behind the consonant. The vowel in front of the consonant now has a short sound.

Rules 48 -54 are more advanced suffix rules.

RULE 48. If there is only one consonant at the end of a one-syllable base word, usually the consonant is doubled before adding any suffix except *S*, as in cut<u>ting</u> and hop<u>ped</u>.

RULE 49. If *Y* immediately follows a consonant at the end of a two-syllable base word, and the suffix does not begin with *I*, change the *Y* to *I* when the suffix is added as in bab<u>ies</u> and sill<u>iest</u>.

RULE 50. If the base word ends with the vowels *AY, OY* or *UY*, the *Y* is usually not changed to *i* before a suffix is added as in pla<u>y</u>ed, to<u>y</u>s, and bu<u>y</u>ing.

RULE 51. The suffix *EST* is a syllable. It has the short *e* sound, as in lar<u>gest</u> and happi<u>est</u>.

RULE 52. Suffix *ER* is a syllable and has the sound as in read<u>er</u> and bak<u>er</u>.

RULE 53. Suffix *LY* is a syllable. It has the sound as in name<u>ly</u> and close<u>ly</u>.

RULE 54. Suffix *FUL* is a syllable. Suffix *FUL* has the sound as in cup<u>ful</u>, bucket<u>ful</u>.

Definition: A *compound* word is two base words joined together to make one word. Both base words must keep all the letters of each word, such as <u>into</u>, <u>something</u>. Both base words must be complete words on their own such as <u>base</u> and <u>ball</u>, <u>key</u> and <u>board</u>.

Definition: A *contraction* is two words joined together, with one or more letters left out, usually from the second word as in <u>haven't</u>, <u>would've</u>.

Rules 55-63 are punctuation rules.

RULE 55. A period(.) is like a stop sign. It tells the reader to stop for a short pause and that a thought has been completed. It is read as if something is being told.

RULE 56. A capital letter always begins a sentence.

RULE 57. A sentence is a complete thought with a period at the end.

RULE 58. A comma (,) tells the reader to make a short pause, a shorter pause than for a period. A thought has not been completed yet.

RULE 59. A colon (:) usually tells the reader that a list is coming right after the colon.

RULE 60. An exclamation mark (!) tells the reader to read as if surprised.

RULE 61. A question mark (?) tells the reader a question is being asked and the tone of his/her voice goes up at the end of the question.

RULE 62. A set of quotation marks (" ") around one or more words, lets the reader know that someone is talking. The quotation marks are like two hands cupped around what is being said.

RULE 63. An *'s* after a name or thing often means something belongs to that name or thing.

Silly Stories to Make Phonics Fun and Easier to Remember

(Listed in the order of first presentation in the book.)

C Sounds of S and K, pages 54 and 145

Silly Story:

The letter C had no sound of its own, poor C. C was so sad and tried so hard to make a sound of its own. Then C remembered a story Momma Cat had read. It was about a cat who copied the sounds of other animals. Here is the story. "First Copy Cat copied the sound of a rooster, then a pig, a horse, and a mule. Next he walked into the forest and copied the sound of a bird and a squirrel."

Letter C thought, mmmmmm . . . maybe I could be a Copy Cat and copy other letter sounds. "I'll ask my best friends, S and K if I can copy their sounds." Sure enough! Both S and K wanted to share their sounds. S said that whenever C had an E, I or Y following it, C could copy its soft sound . . . ssss (as in the word soft.) K thought that was a good idea, so he said C could also copy its sound if an E, I or Y didn't follow C. C gave S and K a big smile, a big thank you, and a big hug. C was a happy Copy Cat. K and S were happy they could help C.

Introduction to G, N, S, W, Y Sounds, page 56

Silly Story:

The letters G, N, S, W, and Y each have their own sounds, but sometimes they think just one sound is rather boring. They wanted to have a second sound also. So they often got together with other letter pals to do unusual, creative, and interesting things. Let's hear their silly stories.

G Sounds of G and J, pages 56 and 153

Silly Story:

The letter G liked the plan that S and K had to help C. G had always admired the sound of J, so G asked J if he could copy the same idea. G explained the plan. If G had an E, I, or Y following it, J would let G make its J sound. J agreed to the plan, but only if G would make its own hard sound when other letters were following it. G happily agreed. But I'll tell you a secret! The plan doesn't always work for G. I wonder why?

NG and NK Sounds, pages 57 and 165

Silly Story:

Another unusual thing about G . . . some of the time when G follows N, they are both so shy, it sounds like N and G are both beginning to swallow their sounds. Listen carefully to hear N and G beginning to swallow their sounds. Listen . . . si<u>ng</u>. Now say the word sing. "Si<u>ng</u>".

But let me tell you, K sure isn't shy when it follows N. K just goes right ahead and says its own sound while shy N still begins to swallow its sound. Listen carefully to hear N begin to swallow its sound while K blurts out its sound. Listen . . . thi<u>nk</u>. Now say the word think. "Thi<u>nk</u>".

S Sounds of SH, SE and SU, page 59

Silly Story:

S liked its own sound. It sounded like a snake's sound-SSS. But S had a problem. When it was at the end of a word, E sometimes tagged right behind him, begging S to make the sound of Z. −ZZZ. S finally asked Z for permission to make the Z sound when E tagged along behind it. Z said, "OK, S use the Z sound when E tags along behind and begs to hear ZZZ, but only at the end of a word." That solved S's problem with E.

When U found out that S got permission to make the sound of Z when E tagged along, U thought, "Mmm, . . . maybe S can sometimes make my favorite sound, too . . . SH." So U asked S if it could make the

SH sound when it tagged along. "<u>S</u>ure," said S, "but only some of the time. "And I just made the SH sound!"

AW, EW, and OW Sounds, page 60
Silly Story:

W liked making its own sound and usually did it when it was the first letter in a word. However, being rather musical, W liked hearing different sounds.

One day W noticed that the vowel letters A, E and O often walked in front of it. W thought it would be fun if A, E and O made some new sounds along with it. After discussing it together A, E and O said when one of them walked in front of W they <u>would</u> make a new sound with W.

So when W saw A, E, or O in front of it, the two of them made new sounds like aw as in <u>saw</u>, EW as in n<u>ew</u>, OW as in h<u>ow</u> and OW as in sh<u>ow</u>. The sounds were musical to W.

Sound of Long I, AY Sound of Long A, page 61
Silly Story:

Y loved being at the beginning and the ending of words. Y made its own sound at the beginning of words like in its favorite color yellow, but it was very difficult to make that sound at the end of words. I and E decided to give Y a wonderful gift.

Since I got lonely at the end of a short word, I said Y could take its place and make I's long sound. E said Y could take its place at the end of a longer word and make E's long sound. Y loved the gift so much, it gave E and I a hug. A was feeling left out, so Y told A it could be in front of it sometimes, and then Y would take a rest and let A sing out its own long A sound. A gave Y a hug.

X Sound of KS and Z, page 64
Silly Story:

Just like Copy Cat C, the letters X and Q had <u>no</u> sound of their own. After they saw that K and S helped Copy Cat C, they too tried to get some help. They found K, S, W, and Z fishing off the dock. After X and Q fished with K, S, W, and Z for awhile, they told them they needed to have help making a sound. All the letters wanted to help.

Z said it didn't get to use its sound much and would X like to use its sound whenever X was at the beginning of a word? "Yes, Yes," said happy X, making its new sound Z, Z, Z.

K and S said X could copy their sounds, too, if X smooshed them together to make its new sound. X tried it. "KS, KS." X liked the new sound of KS. No other letter had a sound like that! X danced around singing its new sound over and over
. . . "KS, KS, KS".

QU Sound of KW, page 65

Silly Story:

Now it was time to help Q. K really liked the smooshed sound of KS that X got, so K told W that smooshed together <u>they</u> would make a nice KW sound for Q. They knew that Q was forgetful, so they asked the letter U to follow Q in every word it was in, helping Q remember its new smooshed sound of KW. And that's why you always find the letter U following the letter Q. And that's why Q always remembers its smooshed sound, KW, KW, KW.

TH and WH Voiced and Unvoiced Sounds, page 71

Silly Story:

TH and WH sometimes got laryngitis. (You know what that is -- when your voice doesn't make any sound, but your mouth still says it with air.)

Well, TH could get laryngitis a lot when it was at the end of a word, but TH <u>could</u> have it happen to it when it was any place at all in a word. When it didn't have laryngitis it used its voice.

WH got laryngitis most of the time at the beginning of a word. It, too, used its voice whenever it didn't have laryngitis.

CH and SH Unvoiced Sounds, page 73

Silly Story:

The letters CH and SH noticed how confused TH and WH were with their rules, so they decided to make simpler rules for themselves. Both CH and SH had laryngitis, so they had to find sounds that didn't use voices.

CH who loved trains, decided it would use a loud sound like the steam engine of a train saying CH-CH-CH-CH.

SH chose to use a quieter sound, like SH-SH-SH. So now CH tiptoes around so quietly, as if someone is sleeping, saying SH-SH-SH-SH.

CK Sound, page 74

Silly Story:

Since K was nice enough to let C copy its sound so often, C promised K that when they were together, it wouldn't copy K's sound at all, and that K could do all the talking. So when we see CK go along together, we hear only K making its sound.

PH Sound of F, page 75

Silly Story:

P and H were only able to get together for a few words, so they wanted to make one of their favorite sounds when they were together. They both agreed F had their favorite sound. They just loved to hear F's sound. Off they went to see if F would let them make its lovely sound. F overheard them talking and felt very honored that P and H wanted to use its sound. Of course he let them use it. So now whenever you see PH walking together remember, they make the sound of F.

Short O Sound of AH, page 86

Silly Story:

A little O shaped doughnut watched while the other doughnuts were put into hot grease. They looked so nice when they came out. Finally it was little O's turn. Ouch, the grease was so hot! Little O didn't have to stay there long before it was taken out of the pan. When little O came out of the hot grease it felt so good it sighed, "AH". From then on little O kept the AH sound as its short sound.

Single and Only Vowel in Middle of Short Word, pages 103 and 105

Silly Story:

Each vowel, A, E, I, O, or U, feels so comfortable when it's the only vowel in the word, and there are consonants on both sides of it. When that happens, the vowel purrs its happy, comfortable short sound.

Single and Only Vowel at End of Short Word, pages 109 and 111

Silly Story:

Whenever a vowel is all by itself in a very short word and is at the end of the word, it is so proud it says its own name, which is its long sound.

Y at the end of a very short word has traded places with I who is too lonely at the end, but Y still uses the sound of long I.

Single Rule in Short Vowel with E at End of Word, page 117

Silly Story:

E loves to practice its jumping skills. E needs a running start, so it can only practice its jumping skills when it is at the end of word. E has a lot of trouble jumping over two consonants, so when there's only one consonant to jump over, E takes a running jump, there it goes, right over the consonant. E lands right on the only other vowel in the word and makes the vowel say its name. (That's the vowel's long sound.) Then E goes back to the end of the word. It loves it there, because it can rest silently.

By the way, no matter how hard E practices, it hardly ever manages to jump over two consonants in front of it. It doesn't make any difference though, if there are one, two or three consonants in front of the other vowel in the word.

Single and Only Vowel at Beginning of Short Word, page 119

Silly Story:

Whoopee! The vowel letter notices it is the only vowel in the word and it got to be the first letter in the word. Thank goodness, E is not at the end wanting to hop over the consonant and change it to its long sound! The vowel is feeling so comfortable and happy that it purrs its short sound.

The vowel doesn't care how many vowels are behind it.

AI and AY Sounds of Long A, page 121

Silly Story:

Remember how A and Y are sometimes together at the end of a word. And how Y told A it could say its long sound? Well, sometimes AY got put into the middle of a word. Y wanted out of there! It was too crowded for Y!

Remember how I said it didn't want to be at the end of a word because it was lonely? Well, I told Y whenever it was crowded into the middle of a word, it would be happy to take its place among lots of letter. And I still let A say its long sound.

OW Sound as in How, page 122

Silly Story:

O and W both take so much room when they are together, that they often bump into each other. You can hear them make the sound, "OW!"

OR Sound, page 125

Silly Story:

The letter R is usually bossy to the vowel in front of it. For instance, R makes the O change its sound, so R's sound is heard better. Then R's nickname is Bossy R.

ER, IR and UR Sound, page 125

Silly Story:

Remember about the letter R usually being Bossy R to the vowel in front of it. Well, when E, I or U are in front of Bossy R, it makes them change their sound so R's sound is heard better so ER, IR and UR sound a little bit like a dog's growl. Oh, that Bossy R!

AL and ALK Sounds, page 127

Silly Story:

When A and L walk together with A going first, A gets shy and says "Ah . . . " Sometimes L makes its regular sound, but sometimes L is speechless. Sometimes K tags along behind A and L. K likes to make its sound, so L is happy to have K there, especially when L is speechless.

Add Suffix ES to a Base Word with the Sound of O, S, SH, CH and J at the End, page 133

Silly Story:

One morning E saw O, S, SH, CH and J chatting together about how much S, SH, CH and J sounded alike. When they invited E to join them, E tried sounding each of their sounds. "What a grand discovery you have made!" he said with pride. "Yes," they agreed, "It is wonderful, but it also gives us all the same problem. You see, when S is a suffix and wants to come after us when we are in a base word, we all sound awful. Just try it, E." E tried the suffix S on the end of bus--buss, wishs, bunchs and bridges. E noticed the words sounded better when E stayed in bridge before the suffix S was added. E tried itself in the word buses, wishes and bunches. Wow! The faces of S, SH, CH and J beamed with happiness. From then on, when E heard the sound of S, SH, CH and J at the end of a base words he joined with S to make the Suffix ES.

"Do it for me, too, E." pleaded O. Now, O seldom is at the end of a word, but when it is, Suffix S changes its sound, like in the words go and no. Suffix S changed O to a short sound, gos and nos. E certainly would help, but with only the <u>sound</u> of S. From then on, when E saw O at the end of a base word, E joined with S to make the Suffix ES, but with the <u>sound</u> of S.

Add Suffix ES, ED or ING to a Base Word with E at End, page 137

Silly Story:

When E is at the end of a word, it likes being the only vowel there. E doesn't want another vowel to join it at the end of a word, because then E couldn't rest silently. E would have to change its sound.

When suffix ES or ED comes to join E at the end of a word, that puts another vowel, E, next to E. E just wants to rest silently, not to change its sound, so E usually just drops and goes away.

When suffix ING comes to the end of a word to join E, that puts the vowel I next to E. Poor E, it just wants to rest silently, but again E usually just drops and goes away.

EE Sound of Long E, page 155

Silly Story:

The twin vowels, EE were very loyal and helpful to each other. The other letters all knew they would always say the same sound which they had agreed upon. Always EE makes the sound of their name, long E.

EA and Its Four Sounds, page 156

Silly Story:

The vowels EA liked to pretend they were twins like the vowels EE. They even tried to make the same vowel sound of long E like the twins, EE. Most of the time they were able to say the long E sound, too.

But sometimes EA forgot they were pretending to be twins. When that happened they borrowed vowel E's short sound or vowel A's long sound, and for no reason at all! Bossy R noticed this, so sometimes he got in behind EA and made them make his growling ER sound.

OO Short Sound, page 157

Silly Story:

Part I. What does an owl do best at night? You know, don't you? They can really <u>look</u> around and see well. The two letters OO noticed they looked just like the owl's big eyes, so wide open at night.

To show their respect to wise owl, the two letters OO decided that whenever they were together in a word they would make the sound heard in the middle of the word <u>look</u>, because owl loved to look around at night. Say the sound of OO that you hear in look.–OO OO OO."

OO Long Sound, page 158

Silly Story:

Part II. The two letters OO listened to the <u>hoot</u>ing sound the owl made as he watched all the night creatures <u>scoot</u>ing around at night. The two letters OO figured the owl must be talking when he <u>hoot</u>ed. Owl must say things like, "OO, see that mouse! OO, there goes a fox! The two letters OO decided they would make the OO, OO, OO, owl's excited OO sound, as their second sound.

OI and OY Sound, page 158

Silly Story:

Whenever the letters O and I got together, in honor of their pet pig, they made the sound OI, because <u>oink</u> was the sound their pig made. Sometimes the OI got at the end of a word. Remember how lonely I was when it was at the end of a word? Remember the agreement I made earlier with Y?

Well, I asked O if it was OK for Y to help whenever O and I were together at the end of a word since I got so lonely there. "Absolutely OK," said O. "Y is a good friend to both of us". So when you see OI or OY together, they are honoring their pet pig and making the sound heard in <u>oink.</u>

OU and Its Six Sounds, page 161

Silly Story:

OU liked hearing the same Silly Stories you've been hearing. When deciding which sounds to copy, OU really wanted to be different. So OU chose to make five different sounds, more than any other letters. OU was the biggest "Copy Cat" of all the letters, and OU didn't get permission either!

OU copied the sound of OW who both took so much room when they were together, they often bumped into each other? Then they said, "OW!"

OU copied OO's two sounds, because he liked the owl story. Remember the owl's eyes that would <u>look</u>? The two OO's used the sound like in <u>look</u>, OO, OO, OO. The OO's also used the sound of the owl's <u>hoot</u>, OO, OO, OO.

OU copied the short sound of O. Remember the Silly Story for short O? The round O shaped doughnut came out of the hot grease and said, "<u>Ah</u>, that feels good!"?

OU copied the short U sound. The umbrella handle looked like U, and also the word <u>umbrella</u> started with the short sound of U, U, U.

OU now had copied five sounds, just like it meant to. Oh, oh, watch out! Here comes Bossy R right behind OU, making OU say the same sound as the word OR.

That ought to make OU happy. Now OU has six different sounds. Wow! That <u>is</u> different. It doesn't use one sound much more than any other sound; and because OU likes being different, it wants the reader to use the words around it to figure out what sound it is making.

ILD, IND and IGH Sounds, page 167

Silly Story:

Letter I liked its long sound better than its short sound. You see, the igloo that helped it remember its short sound also made I cold. So the letter I put up a big poster asking for letters to fill the job of helping it make its long sound more often.

Letters LD, ND and GH immediately applied for the job. They all had the same idea. If they followed I, they could remind I to make its long sound, but most of the time they wanted to be at the end of a word.

Letter I hired them all. LD and ND insisted they wanted to also make their own sounds. Now whenever you see ILD or IND, especially at the end of a word, you know I will make its long sound, and then the other letters will make their sounds.

GH, however, wanted to remain silent. When you see IGH, usually at the end of words, you will hear only the long I sound.

OW At the End of a Word and OLD Sound, page 169

Silly Story:

Remember the story about crowded OW and its OW! sound? Well, OW figured that if it was at the end of a word, it would have more room. Sure enough, when OW got to the end of the word, it had more room and a better view, too. "Oh, look at that view from the end of the word," OW said. From then on, when OW was at the end of a word, it said, "Oh". LD thought it was so much fun following I, it would see if it could get a second job, following O to help it make its long sound. O liked the idea. Now OLD, usually found at the end of a word, makes the long O sound and then the sounds of the other letters.

OA Sound, page 170

Silly Story:

O and A liked things to be simple. They thought it was great that when good friends EE, and good friends AI and AY were together they had just **one** sound that they always said. Do you remember? They had agreed that the first one got to say his name? Well, O and A couldn't get together very often, but they decided that when they **were** together O would say his name.

AR, WAR, WA, and WOR Sounds, page 173

Silly Story:

Here comes Bossy R again, this time following vowel A, making the new sound AR, like you hear in c<u>ar</u>.

Did you know W sometimes played mischievous tricks, even on Bossy R? When W saw AR following it, W loved to change its sound to OR, like you hear in w<u>ar</u>. Whenever W followed A in a word it tricked the A to say the short O sound like in the word shawl. Oh, that mischievous W. Almost always when W saw OR following it, W used yet another trick. It changed OR into the sound of ER like in the word work. Do you think maybe W doesn't like to be followed by AR, A, or OR?

GN, KN and WR Sounds, page 175

Silly Story:

The letters G and K were sometimes pushy to be first in line, especially if N was already there. N told G and K it didn't mind if they wanted to be first, but they couldn't be pushy and that G and K would have to be silent when they were in front of it. N would still be making its own N sound.

Remember mischievous W? Well, he saw G and K get away with being pushy in line, so he tried the same thing with the letter R. He pushed to be first in line, right in front of R. R told W it didn't mind, but W would have to be silent so R could make its own sound.

AU Sound, page 176

Silly Story:

Remember how W thought it would be fun if A, E and O made some new sounds along with it? And how A, E and O agreed that when one of them walked in front of W they <u>would</u> make a new sound with W. Remember that AW made the sound you hear in s<u>aw</u>?

Well AW said since AU wasn't in words very often, it could sometimes make the same sound as AW.

Blend Sounds, page 177

Silly Story:

The consonants all liked to sing. Some of them had such close friends that they teamed together to make just one sound. You probably remember them and their sounds: ch, sh, th, ck, wh, ng, ph, kn, gn, wr.

The rest of the time the consonants all–(well, all but h and k) chose to keep their own individual sound. When they sang, you could hear their individual sounds, but they really liked smooshing their sounds together. There are so many consonants, they could make lots of new sounds such as bl, cl, pl, fl, gl, sl, br, cr, pr, fr, gr, dr, tr, sc, sk, sm, sn, sp, sw, st, squ, scr, str, spl, spr, mp, nd, nk, ft, nt, tch and nch. Lovely!

Y At the End of a Longer Word, page 187

Silly Story:

Y really liked being uncrowded at the end of words, but when the words got longer, Y felt scared, like it was hanging over a cliff. "EEEE!" Y cried out every time. After awhile Y became more used to hanging on the end of a longer word, but from habit Y still cried out EEEE. Vowel E said that it was fine for Y to use its sound when it was hanging from the end of a longer word.

Add Suffix EST, ER, LY or FUL to a Base Word with E at End, pages 196 and 216

Silly Story:

Remember when E is at the end of a word, it likes being the only vowel there and doesn't want another vowel to join it at the end of a word? E wants to rest silently, and it doesn't want to change its sound.

When suffixes ES, ED, ING, EST or ER comes to join E at the end of a word, that puts another vowel, E, next to E. E just wants to rest silently, not to change its sound, so E usually just quietly drops and goes away.

Sometimes LY or FUL comes to the end of a word to join E. To have a consonant next to E was just fine, so E often stayed with LY and FUL.

Doubling Consonants Before Adding a Suffix, page 210

Silly Story:

The base words that had one vowel in the middle and ended with one consonant had a very serious meeting. They didn't know how to protect their vowel. They moaned, "If the suffix is removed, E will get in there real fast to hop over the one consonant and make the vowel say its name. That would change us into a different base word!"

"We know what to do," volunteered the consonant at the word's end.

"We'll just double ourselves when a suffix is added. E can't jump over two consonants, so he won't get in there real fast. After E has given up, we can un-double ourselves. You base words will be safe then."

And that is why a single ending consonant sometimes doubles itself before a suffix is added.

Change Y at End of the Word to I When a Suffix Is Added, page 210

Silly Story:

Remember how Y likes to be at the end of a word. When a suffix joins a base word, Y calls for I to come, because it is feeling very crowded now that it's no longer at the end of the word. I comes bouncing right along to take its place in the middle of the word.

Once in awhile I is at the beginning of the suffix, so Y has to stay in the word. At least I is right there with Y trying to make Y feel better.

Base Words Ending with AY, OY, UY When a Suffix is Added, page 211

Silly Story:

Y is really a very important letter, with so many jobs to do. Sometimes he makes a sound with AY, OY or UY. Usually Y is with those letters at the end of a word.

When a suffix comes to join a word where AY, OY or UY are at the end, Y doesn't leave. Y just grits his teeth and sticks with his friends. Otherwise their sounds would change, and he would feel terrible.

A Story:
The Living Pipe Cleaner

1. The city engineers couldn't figure out how to solve the problem.

2. The drainage pipes were old and dirty. It took a long time for water to drain through them.

3. When it rained, the city streets often flooded because the pipes couldn't drain much water at a time. Those dirty old drainage pipes caused other problems, too.

4. Cars stalled. Buildings got water in them. The city's citizens didn't want to go shopping. Parents wouldn't send their children to school.

5. The engineers tried to use their big expensive equipment to clean the pipes, but the equipment wouldn't fit in the pipes. They called the plumber to try his rotary drill, but it wasn't long enough.

6. The pipes were two blocks long, much too long. What could they use? How could they clean the pipes? They asked for ideas from the citizens.

7. The second grade class at Elbert School thought their pet ferret might help.

8. They had noticed their furry pet liked to get in dark places and go exploring. The class wanted to volunteer their ferret to crawl through the pipe, but they didn't want to lose him. They had a problem solving session.

9. The class decided to tie a strong twine onto their ferret's collar and one-half of the class would quietly put him in the pipe's entrance. The other half of the class would go to the pipe's exit with

the ferret's favorite food and call to the ferret. The city engineers would have to help with the rest of the plan.

10. One city engineer told the class it just <u>couldn't</u> work, but the rest of the city engineers liked the class' idea. They busily prepared to help the second grade class. The next day a big crowd gathered to see how the plan would work.

11. Just as planned, the ferret slipped right into the entrance of the long, dark pipe. The second graders at the exit called to their pet. The little ferret scooted along the two-block-long pipe toward the second graders, exploring all the way to the exit.

12. Out the ferret popped, dragging the twine behind it. The little ferret wasn't even dirty! While it gobbled its favorite food, the workers detached the twine.

13. The workers at the pipe's exit informed the workers at the pipe's entrance that the ferret made it through the pipe with the twine still attached. Workers at the entrance attached a very long strong rope onto the strong twine. The workers at the exit, pulled the twine through the pipe until they got the strong rope. They informed the workers at the entrance that they had the rope. The workers at the entrance now attached a cable onto the strong rope.

14. With a machine, the workers at the exit pulled the stronger rope with the cable behind it, all the way to the pipe's exit. With their new telephones, they informed the workers at the entrance that they had the cable. The workers at the entrance attached a huge stiff round wire brush, a little larger than the pipe's diameter.

15. At the pipe's exit, three husky workers were connecting the end of the cable to the front of a strange looking machine. The machine roared as it started. It's operator slowly backed up, backing up as the machine pulled and tried to turn the cable round and round. Suddenly the machine lurched, sputtered, and came to a dead stop. The operator couldn't get it started again.

16. The city engineers got their heads together to figure out what to do. The workers got their heads together to figure out what to do. The second graders got their heads together to figure out what to do. They even asked Tommy's dad to join them for awhile. Then the city engineers, the workers, the second graders, and

Tommy's dad <u>all</u> got their heads together. They had decided to try a different machine.

17. The cable was attached to the back of Tommy's dad's big farm tractor. It roared to life with a forward jerk. Slowly the tractor moved down one block and down the second block, pulling behind it the large rotating cable.

18. The watching crowd saw a huge growing pile of leaves, twigs, rusty scales and dirt forming on the ground outside the pipe's exit until finally the big round wire brush came out. The plan had worked. The turning brush had pushed debris out of the pipe as the tractor pulled it forward.

19. Tommy's dad heard the citizens cheer from two blocks away. The next day the mayor gave the second grade class a "Great Problem Solvers" plaque and each student a big blue ribbon. He gave the ferret a year's supply of its favorite food and a pipe to explore. The words, "The Living Pipe Cleaner" were engraved on the pipe.

BIBLIOGRAPHY

Arizona Republic, "Phonics drills best way to make kids better readers, study says," May 5, 1996.

Colvin, Richard Lee, *Los Angeles Times*, "Reading Blues — Teachers Say They Must Water Down Classes Because Students Lack Basic Skills," May 17, 1998.

Dolch, Edward, "A Basic Sight Vocabulary," *Elementary School Journal* XXXVI, No. 5, 1936.

Duff, Christina, *The Wall Street Journal*, "ABCeething – How Whole Language Became a Hot Potato In and Out of Academia," October 30, 1996.

Flesch, Rudolph, *Why Johnny Can't Read*, Harper and Row, N.Y., 1955.

Fry, Edward, "A Frequency Approach to Phonics," *Elementary English*, Vol. 6, 1964.

Hall, Katherine L., *Reading Stories for Comprehension Success: Primary Level*, Center for Applied Research in Education, Prentice-Hall, NY, 1997.

Kiester, Edwin Jr. and Sally Valente Kiester, "Does Your Child Have a Learning Disability?" *Reader's Digest*, August 1997.

New York Times, "End 'reading wars' with hybrid teaching methods, report urges," *Minneapolis Star Tribune*, March 19, 1998.

Palmaffy, Tyce, "See Dick Flunk," *Policy Review*, Nov/Dec 97, Issue 86.

Raffaele, Paul, "Saving the Snow Tiger," *Reader's Digest*, July 1998.

Rieben, Laurence and Charles A. Perfetti, *Learning to Read: Basic Research and Its Implications*, Lawrence Erelbaum Assoc., N.J., 1991.

Snow, Catherine, "'It's Time to End the Reading Wars,'" *National Education Association Journal*, May 1998.

INDEX

To order additional copies of

YOU
Can Teach
Someone to Read

purchase from your local bookstore,

go online to

www.youcanteachsomeonetoread.com

or contact

GLoBooks Publishing LLC

PMB 433
2487 S. Gilbert Road #106
Gilbert, AZ 85295
email: globkspub@aol.com
phone: 602-321-7421

About the Author

After retiring from 33 years of classroom teaching and administrating, Lorraine Peoples wrote *You Can Teach Someone to Read*. It was soon awarded the best how-to-book in its category. She has since given over 150 workshops, seminars and book signings at bookstores (mostly Barnes & Noble), libraries and literacy groups throughout the country. Through her website, www.youcanteachsomeonetoread.com, she has advised hundreds of individuals internationally with their reading concerns. Lorraine worked with staff at The Phoenix Lodestar Resource Center to develop a viable program for homeless adults and trained volunteers to use the program. In various settings, she has trained youth and adults how to teach others to read. She volunteer teaches reading for some ELL students in Holmes Elementary School, Mesa, Arizona.

Author, Lorraine Peoples, has degrees in elementary education, and elementary curriculum and instruction, and a certification in elementary administration. During her thirty-three years of teaching elementary age children reading and other subjects, she also gave fifty-two workshops to educators on subjects including reading, science, team teaching and/or individualizing. In addition she trained twelve student teachers and mentored eight first year teachers.

For sixteen years, the author taught first through fifth in Des Moines and Marshalltown, Iowa public schools and was active on various curriculum committees. The next seventeen years she taught in private schools in Phoenix and Paradise Valley, Arizona. While at Phoenix Country Day School she was Acting Dean of Lower School for a semester and active on curriculum and evaluation committees. At Tesseract School, she was also Elementary Program Director for several years.

Lorraine founded libraries in Cement, Oklahoma and Liscomb, Iowa, and trained corps of women in service clubs to operate them. She is listed in various "Who's Who" Editions from 1986 to the present. Lorraine and her husband, Graydon, live in Chandler, Arizona.